LESSONS FROM A HEADHUNTER... WITH HEART

Spiritual and Practical Keys to Navigating (and Surviving!) Job Change

PATRICIA A. COMEFORD, J.D.
WITH GINA SAUER, J.D.

LESSONS FROM A HEADHUNTER…WITH HEART!

ISBN 10: 1-59298-137-2
ISBN 13: 978-1-59298-137-3

Library of Congress Catalog Number: 2005911216

Book design and typesetting: Mori Studio
Cover design: Mori Studio

Printed in the United States of America

First Printing: April 2006

08 07 06 05 6 5 4 3 2 1

Beaver's Pond Press, Inc.

7104 Ohms Lane, Suite 216
Edina, MN 55439
(952) 829-8818
www.BeaversPondPress.com

To order, visit *www.BookHouseFulfillment.com* or call 1-800-901-3480. Reseller and special sales discounts available.

Table of Contents

The "Planning" Lessons

The "Doing" Lessons

INTRODUCTION

A HEADHUNTER★ WRITING ABOUT SPIRITUAL principles? You're probably thinking, "You must be joking."

I'm not.

I didn't start out as a headhunter. In college, I had absolutely no clue what I wanted to be when I grew up. So what did I do? Like lots of others, I decided to go to law school. After all, everyone kept saying, "You can do anything with a law degree!" So after graduating and finding out it really *wasn't* all that easy to do anything with a law degree right out of school, I accepted a job as a litigator with a law firm. And I hated it. There I was in a well-respected law firm, making good money, and I just hated it. I felt like I was fighting all day and all night, and it was a big waste of time and energy. Not that the practice of law isn't a wonderful profession—I help people find jobs in law everyday. It just wasn't the right profession for *me*.

So after two years of gutting it out, and after sinking into a deep depression, I decided to do something about it. I looked at all kinds of jobs and found that nobody (aside from other lawyers) could understand why I was so unhappy. People would say, "You went to law school to be a lawyer—what do you mean you don't want to practice law?" or, "You spent all that time going to law school and now you don't want to use your law degree? What a waste!" *What they were all really saying was, "What's wrong with you?"*

In addition, while the job search community was willing to help me find another job as a lawyer, nobody was too interested in helping me change career paths. That, I quickly learned, I had to do on my own. So I went on what can only be described as a spiritual journey and uncovered many lessons along the way—much of which I will share with you in the following pages.

After six months of market research, study, and repeated soul-searching, I realized that what I truly wanted to do was start a business. I also knew that I wanted to use my background in law, and I knew that there were lots of unhappy lawyers out there who, like me, had made some wrong career choices. So I focused on filling an unmet need in the industry—helping lawyers find the right job. Getting the business off the ground was a long and arduous process, and I made my share of mistakes along the way, but I have never regretted my decision. The business has expanded and now includes career coaching, as well as permanent and project staffing for lawyers, paralegals and litigation support professionals, but at its core it is about helping clients find happiness and satisfaction in their work—something I find tremendously satisfying.

The idea for this book came to me when someone asked me how I "spent my time during the day." A light bulb went on. I realized that I was doing a whole lot more than calling on clients and building a business; I spent the great majority of my day helping people navigate not only the practical elements of the job search process (i.e., change), but the emotional and spiritual as well. I also realized that when I walked down the job search aisles of bookstores, I saw very little that helped people with those issues, although they are the hardest parts!

So unlike the many "how to write a résumé and cover letter" books out there, this book is all about helping you move beyond your barriers, whether self-imposed or imposed by others. It is about helping you create the work life you want, not just get a job. And if you let it, you will find that a job search can teach you powerful lessons that not only bolster your professional development, but transform you. It is my sincere wish and prayer that at least some of the lessons in this book will resonate with you and enable you to find the fulfilling work you so richly deserve.

*I've never been offended by the term headhunter and I hope you won't be either! In today's world, the polite term is "search consultant."

A Helpful Way To Use This Book

This is a thought book, one of those little books you can take with you wherever you go or keep on your nightstand. Its mission is to help you make the sometimes painful process of changing jobs into a *life-transforming* experience. In fact, it is my firm belief that the transformation process is the hidden treasure in a job change. As you'll see, the lessons are about much more than job hunting or writing a résumé—they're about life itself.

If you're in the midst of a job search and/or struggling with whether to leave your job, take a look at the table of contents and open to the topic that grabs you. There are no rules here, and no right or wrong way to read this book – you write the rules. But do me one favor: When you're reading, envision yourself in the most comfortable place you can think of – your own living room, your office, your kitchen – and imagine that you and I are having a private conversation. Imagine that we are having a personal coaching session together.

Most books on careers focus only on how to write a résumé and cover letter, how to set goals, or how to deal with financial planning. Those are certainly pieces to the puzzle, but in my fifteen years of working with candidates and clients, I have found that they are not typically the hardest parts. Consequently, most of the lessons in this book focus on emotional and spiritual challenges we face in our careers and job searches and life itself. However, because the practical how-tos are an integral, inescapable part of any career search, I have included some of that advice as well. Those lessons (or particular bits of advice within lessons) are indicated by the "nuts and bolts alert" symbol, which looks like this:  .

Each lesson draws on what I've learned from working with job seekers and employers, as well as my own life-transforming experience. In fact, many of the lessons I share with you are ones I keep learning over and over at deeper levels. Nonetheless, I have been careful not to make this book about me and not to tell stories about my clients that might invade their privacy. Given that I am a bit of an impatient type myself, I also want this book to be fast and to the point.

The lessons are grouped into what I think are the four main phases of the job search journey: 1) CONTEMPLATING a career change, 2) OVERCOMING the obstacles and barriers you place in front of yourself, 3) laying the groundwork and PLANNING to start the more formal part of your job search, and then 4) actually DOING the things you need to do to conduct an effective search. Before each set of lessons, you will find a very brief introduction to help you understand what to expect from that phase of your journey; there is also a short "recap" at the end of each set of lessons that will allow you to reflect upon, and synthesize, what you've learned so far. You will also notice the "jump" symbol in some lessons: or . It indicates that an important theme discussed in that lesson is developed more fully in another lesson; readers interested in exploring the topic in more depth are directed where to look.

At the end of each lesson, you'll find a "CAREER COMFORT," a little nugget of wisdom that can get you through the toughest of times in your journey. I discovered their power in my own transformation process. It has been an amazing lesson for me to learn just how one's entire outlook can shift as a result of one powerful phrase. Sometimes that nugget is a quote, sometimes it's an affirmation or spiritual principal, sometimes it's advice that was given to me by a trusted advisor, coach or parent. Use them and use them often; they will pull you through some of your tougher moments. You won't believe how comforting, supportive and powerful they are.

Finally, because of my admittedly spiritual approach to the journey of job searching, I make references throughout this book to the need to trust in your Higher Power, and to believe that your Higher Power will bring you the right job at the right time. I was raised Catholic; while that particular ideology is no longer an integral part of my belief system today, I firmly believe that there is a "Higher Power" at work in all our lives. Because the spiritual aspects of a job search transcend any particular religious doctrine or background, you should feel free to assign whatever meaning to "Higher Power" that is consistent with your own belief system.

Lastly, in the words of the esteemed author Joseph Campbell, *follow your bliss.* Enjoy your life-transforming journey and God bless.

Welcome to The CONTEMPLATING Lessons

It begins as the smallest seed of an idea in the back of your brain, then it starts to grow. It's not long before it is a nagging thought that becomes impossible to ignore. You know the one: "I'm not happy in this job." From the first moment that vague thought creeps into your mind, until the moment when you are seated at your new desk in your new office, you will feel like you have many miles to go and much work to do. Perhaps you will ultimately decide to move to another, but similar, job; perhaps it will mean a more radical career change. Or maybe, you won't leave your job at all, but will make changes to make your current position a more fulfilling one. Either way, the journey must start with soul-searching, with you being honest with *you*.

The CONTEMPLATING lessons are here to help you through that initial thought process, to guide your thinking as you begin to broach this topic with yourself, and to provide a source of strength, affirmation and support. This initial contemplation phase may take weeks, months or even years. Any of those timelines are natural, but if you've experienced dissatisfaction in your current position, you owe it to yourself to begin the exploration process now.

Your journey has begun…

LESSON 1

You're Never Stuck

YOU ARE NEVER STUCK. DO YOU BELIEVE that? My own transformation experience and more than fifteen years of helping others create new career paths have taught me that the single most potent factor influencing career success is what we believe about ourselves. I'm not talking only about the cognitive beliefs we hold, but also the spiritual and emotional beliefs we carry with us. Simply put, you can't experience a transformation if somewhere inside yourself, either cognitively, spiritually or emotionally, you believe that you're stuck.

So as part of your transformation journey, it's crucial to dig out your conscious and unconscious beliefs. I used to think this kind of talk was fluff, but it's not. What we believe about the money we can make, the careers we can have, or the gifts and abilities we offer the world, actually creates our reality. If you believe you're stuck, then you are. If you believe you won't ever be wealthy, then you won't. You create your reality and have to take responsibility for what happens.

Take a minute and embrace how much power that gives you!

I'm not saying it's impossible to find a job if you continue to believe that you're stuck or somehow limited. You can; you have before. But until you change that belief, the chances are good that you'll put yourself into another situation where you feel stuck and unfulfilled. You'll repeat the pattern that's brought you to this point in your life.

Changing your patterns of thought and action is not easy; changing a core belief like, "I'm stuck" or, "I'm not worthy," takes more than just changing your thoughts. It takes gut-wrenching, hard work, and it's often scary and uncomfortable. After all, you are messing with your foundation! You can comfort yourself through this fear by remembering that these foreign feelings are natural and that they are a sign that you're in the process of healing and transforming.

Some of my clients find it helps to think of themselves as what some spiritual teachers call "Compassionate Witnesses" to their own transformation. As a Compassionate Witness, their job is to step back and compassionately pay attention to their thoughts and actions—not only how they talk to themselves and others, but also what they are thinking. I encourage you to try it. And while you do this, be gentle with yourself. Don't beat yourself up or judge yourself—it won't get you anywhere. All you have to do is pay attention to your thoughts. When you see that you're thinking that you are stuck, you can then decide to do things differently.

Exercise

To begin the process, ask yourself the following questions:

- Do you believe your work situation is the product of choice or chance?
- Do you believe that you're stuck?
- If so, what do you believe about being stuck?
- Do you want it to be that way?
- How *do* you want it to be?
- What other thoughts or beliefs would you need to change, in order for you to accept that you are not stuck?

Career Comfort:

Because I have a choice in what I believe, I am not stuck. I take care of myself, I have the freedom to make choices, and I have the ability to create the work life I want.

LESSON 2

Stop Hating Your Job

HATING YOUR JOB WON'T HELP YOU FIND something better.

Really.

I know. It can be hard not to hate your job, but don't fall into that trap. I hated my job as a lawyer from day two, and I stayed there, hating it and telling everyone that I hated it, for two whole years! All that hating just made me feel stuck and very miserable.

We see this phenomenon in other areas of our life. Dr. John Gottman, founder of the Gottman Institute, has performed three decades of research on couples' relationships. Gottman's research has uncovered that four kinds of negativity, which he calls "the four horsemen of the apocalypse," when regularly engaged in, literally destroy a relationship. These four horsemen include: 1) Criticism, 2) Contempt, 3) Defensiveness, and 4) Stonewalling.

Criticism and contempt are frequently present in individuals thinking about or undergoing a job search. With respect to criticism, it is certainly easier to focus on what's wrong with our employer or boss. Contempt rears its ugly head all sorts of ways, including sarcasm, cynicism, put-downs—any attempt to put the focus on the other individual rather than take responsibility for our situation.

So how do we get past criticism and contempt? Gottman challenges couples to communicate five positive comments for every negative one. (Try it in your relationship; it's not so easy!) I challenge you to try it in your work life.

For me and many of my clients, the spiritual lesson in all of this is that it wasn't until *I* changed—until I stopped criticizing and hating my job—that things began to change.

A second helpful tool in overcoming criticism and contempt in our job search is to bless the job you have, as suggested by Louise Hay in her book, *You Can Heal Your Life.* I know, it feels silly, but do it anyway. If that feels like too much of a stretch, revert to Dr. Gottman's advice: say five good things for every criticism. Surely, there must be some good things to be thankful for in your job: Your paycheck? Your co-workers? The flexibility? The creativity?

As specifically recommended by author Louise Hay, I used to bless my job over and over again, out loud, while I was driving to work. I'd repeat, "Thank you for the job I have." Then I'd thank God for the job having been there when I needed it. I'd say I was choosing to pass the job on to the next person who needed it and I'd wish that person well.

At first, I felt like an idiot practicing this "affirmative self-talk," as I call it. But in a very short time, things started to change. Suddenly I began to have a completely different mindset. I felt a true sense of possibility and my feelings of doom and gloom started to dissipate. I began to feel in control instead of trapped, and I slowly started meeting the people I needed to meet. At the time, I didn't recognize that *I* was changing and transforming—all I knew was that things were starting to turn around for me.

Another step is to write down everything you believe about work. Do you believe that work is just a means to an end? Is it something you just have to tolerate? Can people be happy and thrive in their work?

Follow that up by writing down what you believe about your current job. Are you getting what you want out of your work? If not, what's missing? What parts of your work do you want to take with you? What parts do you want to leave behind? What are your reasons for wanting to make a change?

Finally, write down what you believe about success and failure. Do you believe that success is for everyone or just an elite few? Is success something that's hard won?

Read what you've written and ask yourself if you see any patterns. Is what you've written what you truly internalize and put into practice? If you're like most of us, it probably isn't.

Once you've done that, it's time to write down what you *want* to believe about your work, and what you want to claim from it. Most people find it easier to say what they *don't* want than what they *do* want. Don't worry if that's true for you—knowing what you don't want is an important part of the process as well. You can start there, and then simply turn the negative statement into a positive one. For example, if you start with, "I don't want to work in an environment that stifles my creativity," turn it into, "I want to work in an environment that fosters creativity." Write one succinct (but emotionally powerful!) paragraph.

For you fans of the author Stephen Covey, it may be helpful to think of what you're doing as writing a mission statement. For you fans of the author Gary Zukav, it might be helpful to think of it as identifying the "soul of the job."

When I worked through this process myself, I wrote:

> *I work with people who treat each other with respect. We recognize that blame and backstabbing drain our energy and creativity, and in no way serve our clients. My work allows me to express my creativity, learning, intelligence, and giftedness. I earn fantastic money easily, doing things that I love. My career is filled with abundance, intellectual stimulation and opportunity.*

Notice that I said nothing about job titles or the industry I worked in—all that came later! But the soul of the job, what I wanted from work itself, was there. Initially focus on that—the underlying stuff you most want from your work, and claim it for yourself. To further explore the concept of the "soul of the job," jump to Lesson 25.

CAREER COMFORT:

> *I bless this job and thank my Higher Power for sending it to me when I needed it. I am choosing to lovingly release it and pass it on to the next person who needs it. I now choose to move on to a position that meets my needs and helps me fulfill what is best in me.*

LESSON 3

PEOPLE EVOLVE... AND SO DO CAREERS

REMEMBER HOW EXCITED YOU FELT THE day you applied for your current job, the anticipation you felt after your initial interview, and the great sense of accomplishment and well-being you had when you first sat down at your new desk? You knew this was exactly the right fit for you. So why does the job that you busted your tail to get two or five or twelve years ago suddenly feel so wrong? How could you have been so mistaken about your supposed "dream job"? You weren't—it's called career evolution.

In short, you've outgrown your job. That's not surprising, considering that as human beings we are constantly growing and changing. We buy a starter home fully expecting that as our needs change, we'll upgrade. We outgrow relationships all the time; for many of us, it's hard to imagine being with our high school sweetheart at this point in our lives.

And so it is with jobs. Maybe you've mastered the skills needed for your current job to the point where it's no longer a challenge. Maybe your priorities have shifted and the "soul of the job" is no longer right for you. (See Lesson 25 ➦). Whatever the reason, don't talk yourself out of seeking a new position. If it is in fact time to move on, don't let the fact that you wanted this job so badly or enjoyed it so immensely at an earlier point in your career development stop you. What matters is the here and now.

Similarly, don't let the fact that this is a "great" job by other people's standards influence your decision as to whether it continues to be right for you. Many people hesitate to leave a job they've outgrown because a voice in the back of their mind says, "Lots of people would give anything to have this job; I'd be crazy to leave." Lots of people might, in fact, covet your job…and it may just be time to let them have it, while you move on to something better suited to the person you are right now.

Exercise

- Why did you initially accept your current job?
- What, if anything, has changed about the job since you first accepted it?
- What has changed about you since you first accepted your current job?
- What skills do you possess now that you did not possess (or were not as adept at) when you first took your current job?
- What goals did you want to achieve when you first started your current position?
- Have you achieved them?

Career Comfort:

People grow and change; if my job has not grown with me, I have the ability to choose a job that is right for me now.

LESSON 4

WE MAKE OUR OWN BED

OUR HIGHER POWER HAS GIVEN US FREE will—the gift of choice. We can choose to believe that we're stuck in an unsatisfying job. We can choose to remain unhappy in our work. Or we can choose to create a work life that we want. We can choose to choose!

People who don't exercise the gift of choice consciously when they first choose a career usually have to exercise it later. They find themselves unhappy or unfulfilled in their work. They'll need to move on.

Your choices—the ones you make willingly and the ones you make unwillingly—reflect the career and life lessons you need to learn. Pay attention to them. Don't beat yourself up for having to learn them. Ask yourself: what career and life lessons are you learning right now in your job? Embrace them gently, knowing that you'll take them with you wherever you go.

Many of us subconsciously refuse to exercise the gift of choice in our careers. We may say that we need to make choices but somewhere deep down we refuse to actually make them. We fear that unknown part of ourselves. We whisper terrible things to ourselves—

that we're not as good as we pretend, or that maybe we're not marketable after all.

To overcome our fear and utilize our gift of choice, we have to claim our power. We have to trust once again in our Higher Power and our intuition. This allows us to create the work life we want and, if necessary, make new choices when the career choices we made in the past no longer serve us.

It's extremely helpful to gently remind yourself that if you don't choose, someone else will choose for you. When you choose not to exercise your own free will, you are leaving your career choices to others and to circumstance. Think about it: no one has your best interests at heart more than you do—shouldn't YOU be the one to make the choices that affect you and your career? Would you prefer that your job be the result of a conscious, well thought-out decision on your part... or the result of default?

CAREER COMFORT:

I exercise my free will in my job search because I am in the best position to determine what is right for me.

LESSON 5

LEAVE, STAY... OR SCULPT?

AS I DISCUSSED IN THE INTRODUCTION to this set of lessons, everyone who is on this journey starts with the same, vague feeling: *I'm not happy in my job*. But before summarily deciding that your only option is departure, ask yourself exactly WHAT it is about your job that is causing your dissatisfaction, and WHETHER it could be addressed through some means other than resignation. For example, maybe you like the substance of your job, and feel your company is a good place to work, but a particular supervisor, a coworker, or the commute is the real root of your unhappiness. Can this relationship be worked out, or can you be re-assigned to another department? Is moving closer to work an option for you?

Perhaps you enjoy certain duties in your job but not others. Can your job be re-sculpted to allow you to focus on the areas you feel are your forte? A colleague of mine decided to leave her job because, while she greatly enjoyed her marketing duties, she was entirely burnt out on counseling clients. After discussions with her supervisor and the human resources department, her employer rewrote her job description to focus solely on marketing, and reassigned her counseling duties to other staff members.

Job sculpting has become increasingly common in the marketplace as a matter of pure economics; employers recognize that it is better to realign a valued employee's job and thereby keep her, than to lose her and incur the time and expense of bringing in someone new. As noted by the American College of Healthcare Executives:

> *Since most employees leave due to lack of interest or enjoyment in their work, managers are increasingly turning to job sculpting—tailoring work to align with an employee's life interest. Life interests are emotionally driven interests—not merely hobbies, but rather factors that motivate an employee at his or her core.*

You may be surprised to find your employer is much more open to this option than you think.

The key in making job sculpting happen, however, is to make it easy for your employer to understand what you are asking for. That means that you have to do the work for the employer! One of the most effective ways is to draft a proposal for your employer. If after much soul searching you determine re-sculpting is your best option, Lesson 32 will help you craft that effective proposal.

But what if, after careful introspection, you determine that those aspects of your job that are causing your dissatisfaction cannot be changed? Is it time to go? Not necessarily. We all know that nothing in life is ever perfect—no relationship, no possession, no job. Life is a series of trade-offs; we live with the imperfections because, *in the balance,* the good aspects of the thing in question outweigh the bad. If you are considering leaving, ask yourself what direction the scale tips with respect to your job. Do the positive aspects make up for having an occasionally cranky boss, or a ridiculously long commute? Or have you reached the point where you can't enjoy any of the good parts because the bad ones dominate?

In weighing these factors, it is important to stay tuned to the "ubiquitous golden handcuffs." It's become a cliché that too many people stay in a job that in all other respects is wrong for them, because of one factor alone: their substantial paycheck. If this is a stumbling block for you, be sure to take a look at Lessons 16, 17 and 18.

Exercise

- List those things you really enjoy about your job (duties, people, environment, etc.).
- List those things that, while you don't consider them to be fully positive, you can at least tolerate.
- List those that you feel you can no longer tolerate.
- How do they compare? Are there significantly more in one category than the others?
- Can the items in the negative column be changed?
- Who could help you change them?
- What would have to happen in order for them to change?

Career Comfort:

I have options to consider other than leaving my job immediately.

LESSON 6

Until You're Ready, You're Not Ready

WE JUST TALKED ABOUT THE MANY options you have: leaving, staying or sculpting. What if you choose leaving? Or what if that choice has been made for you? Should you immediately jump into your job search with both feet? Probably not. In my role as a headhunter, I have witnessed many people walk through my office door radiating loss, pain and rejection (particularly after a lay-off or termination). I immediately redirect them to a counselor or a coach, because it's too early for them to start looking for a job.

Yes, the world is full of opportunity, but you have to position yourself correctly to seize it. It's somewhere between difficult and downright excruciating to seize anything when your self-esteem is at rock bottom. Don't torture yourself. Give yourself as much time as you need to heal. I know that can be tough. You *want* to move on...and most of us have economic pressures, and pressure from others, to move on as well.

So don't go out and paper the town with résumés, don't call up all your contacts, and above all, don't succumb to friends telling you "to get out there right away" or offering to call up all their contacts immediately for you. Employers are incredibly perceptive around loss issues; it's actually counterproductive for you to "get out there" before you've worked through those issues. It's important for you to stay in charge. So thank your well-meaning friends for their willingness to help, and let them know you'll be taking them up on their offer to make introductions when the time is right.

In short, don't let your anxiety rule your actions. Give yourself enough time to explore whatever feelings of loss you have. If you've just been let go, give yourself a minimum of three full days to feel what you need to feel. If you're like most of us and need to keep working, set aside a series of evenings or weekends to explore your loss before you start taking action.

You can't put your best foot forward until you've put your loss behind you. Until then, the chip, the hurt, the disappointment or just plain old grief will be visible to prospective employers, and anyone with whom you network, even though you're convinced you're hiding it well.

A colleague of mine once counseled a job seeker who got rejection after rejection following each initial interview, even though her credentials were impeccable and she was normally a very effective communicator. When she finally mustered the courage to ask an interviewer why he had rejected her, he candidly told her, "Even though you chose your words carefully, I could sense how bitter you were toward your last employer. I was concerned that someday you might feel that kind of bitterness toward me."

How will you know when you're ready? You'll know when you're ready because you'll be able to let go of your loss graciously. Recognize that we live in a small world and you don't want to burn bridges, no matter how tempting it is.

Difficult as it may be, as you exit, thank your current employer for having given you such opportunities and wish your employer well.

A final, crucial step in being ready is to forgive yourself. Too often we expend valuable energy beating ourselves up and tormenting ourselves with endless questions about our last job like, "Why did I stay in that job so long?" or, "How could I have gotten myself into a situation like that in the first place?" Don't be so hard on yourself. In spiritual circles it is often said, "When the student is ready, the teacher appears." So beating yourself up is a waste of time that doesn't accomplish anything, and merely hinders you from moving ahead. Remind yourself that, like all relationships, every work relationship constitutes an assignment made by our Higher Power. A work relationship gives us an opportunity to learn not just from the job but from each other. It also presents us with an opportunity to heal our wounds. If you process and embrace "your past assignments," you will know when you are ready.

Career Comfort:

I will know when I am ready and I will wait until then to take appropriate action.

LESSON 7

Do You Stay or Do You Go?

OK, YOU'RE STARTING TO FEEL LIKE YOU might be "ready," as we just discussed in the previous lesson. But what about the timing? Isn't timing everything, as they say? One well-entrenched school of thought posits that it's easier to get a job when you have a job. That may have had some validity in an industrial economy, but it's not a hard-and-fast rule in today's information and service economy. Think about the number of professionals (nurses, doctors, executives, lawyers, accountants) who do temporary work or make their living by consulting. The stigma of not having a job while you are looking for another is, for the most part, going away.

So instead of focusing on what others will think, focus on you. The decision to stay or not to stay in a job while you search for another is a very personal one, and the answer is different for everybody. I have seen way too many people stay in a job that was destroying their spirit and sense of possibility. While they labored on, they attempted to go joyfully out into the job market...but their feelings of powerless and sense of being trapped undermined their search.

On the other hand, some people have been able to use a soul-destroying job as a jumping-off place to find work that was truly satisfying.

In deciding whether to stay or go, ask yourself the following:

- Is this job interfering with your ability to put your best foot forward?
- Is it destroying your spirit?
- Would you feel like a lesser person when networking and interviewing if you didn't have a job?
- Can you afford to leave this job or reconfigure this job if you need to do so?
- Would it make you more anxious to leave or stay?
- Looking for a job is a job in and of itself. Does your current job give you sufficient time and flexibility to effectively network and job seek?

For example, if not having a paycheck would create so much stress that you couldn't focus on your job search, then you should stay. On the other hand, if the job is destroying your mental health or consuming you, and you have some financial breathing room, then by all means get out. In such a case, you may find that leaving your job now, rather than waiting to leave until you have secured another position, is an important act of self-love. And understand that by "self-love" I am not simply referring to a positive emotion. Self-love is a state of being and, more importantly, a state of *action* that leads us to take care of ourselves by removing ourselves from distracting or non-empowering environments.

Remember: employers hire the person that they believe will do the best job, not necessarily the person who's currently employed.

Career Comfort:

I can trust what's right for me, and I can leave my job whenever the time is right for me.

LESSON 8

NEGATIVES ATTRACT

BACK IN LESSON 2, WE TALKED ABOUT the importance of not hating your job. That takes a lot of work and constant reminding, so let's pause for a moment and see how you're doing with that, and take it a step further. The related, but broader, concept of negative thinking will impact every phase of your job search journey. We know that in science (and, some say, in romantic relationships) "opposites attract." But if you are trying to create a positive work life, you will find that negative energy merely attracts more negative energy.

If you participate in complaining to others about your job, gossiping, or blaming your boss and the board, it is important to be aware that you are engaging in a form of negative thinking. By thinking negatively, you're really hurting yourself, not the person or entity you are complaining about. In short, you're giving away your power. You may ultimately choose to participate in this kind of activity, but recognize that by doing so you're choosing to disempower yourself and you're losing control of your career.

One thing that's become clear to me in my work as a headhunter is how negative thinking also does a great job of sabotaging your interviews. I can't tell you how many employers have told me that they chose one candidate over another, in part because of their perception of a candidate's thinking. In today's world, most employers have come to realize that what makes a top-notch performer in a company is *attitude*. For more examples of this, see Lesson 27.

In addressing negativity, I'm not asking you to wear rose-colored glasses. You want to be authentic. It is equally counter-productive to live in denial and pretend that everything is perfect at work when it is not. We need to recognize when there are real problems in our work environment and take steps to correct them, or make the decision to move on to a healthier work environment.

So what I am asking you to do here is to choose your thoughts instead of letting your thoughts—or other people's thoughts—rule you.

To accomplish this:

1. **Decide that with respect to your career, your inner voice is the only one that matters.** You will need to be firm with yourself on this. Turn off the chatter; turn off the gossip; turn off the blame. They only drain your energy. This may mean making the difficult decision to disassociate yourself from certain people. Hold onto your power and gracefully walk away from negative conversation if you have to.
2. **Decide right now to view your career and the changes you're making positively.** Choose not to waste your time and energy on other thoughts. Choose to keep your power!

3. **Remind yourself of the power of a decision.** You can decide to think of things differently than co-workers and when you do, the result is positive experiences. What you focus on grows and increases. So focus on the positive.

Career Comfort:

I choose to say yes to all good, all opportunity, and all blessings. I choose to turn away from my own negativity and the negativity of others.

LESSON 9

PAIN CAN BE A GIFT

YOU'VE DONE A LOT OF HARD WORK AND introspection already in getting to this point in the book, so I think you might be ready now to open yourself up to a concept that takes some getting used to. Believe it or not, the pain that you are feeling can be a good thing. I know that runs counter to everything we've been taught. Society has programmed us to believe that if we feel any kind of pain, the immediate response should be to get rid of it, even before we've really thought through where that pain is coming from. Got a headache? Pop some aspirin. Feeling anxious? Have a cocktail to take the edge off.

What we forget is that pain—both physical and emotional—is there for a reason. It's nature's way of telling us we need to make a change. Pain can be a gift if you use it as a motivator and teacher. It can help you find your life's work. I'm not talking here about tolerating physical abuse, work abuse, invasions of privacy or sexual harassment. Those types of pain are inexcusable and if you experience them you must respect yourself enough to leave, and to take any other appropriate action. What I am referring to is the pain you experience when your job fails to fit with your values and aspirations.

When I was practicing law, the pain was so excruciating that it thrust me into making a career change. It forced me not only to ask myself what made my spirit soar but, perhaps even more importantly, helped me make sure that I did not put myself in the same situation again. What a blessing!

With a lot of work and research, I decided to start a business. I didn't have a dime to my name, owed a ton of money in student loans and had my share of credit card debt. People thought I was nuts and in for a whole lot of even more pain. What they didn't know was how much pain I was already in and what a gift it was to me!

Obviously I'm not saying that pain has to be there in order to change, but if it is, don't be afraid of it. Embrace it but don't wallow in it. Use it as your teacher, knowing that once pain's lessons are taught you will be in a new and better place, one that fits your values and aspirations.

Career Comfort:

Listening to my pain will bring me to a new awareness of my values and aspirations. I have nothing to fear.

LESSON 10

We All Have an Inner Career Coach

If the concepts we've talked about so far still seem a little scary, remember, throughout this process you will have your own inner career coach to guide you. Yes, you really do have one. It's that quiet voice inside that some people call intuition and others call Divine Intelligence, Grace or their Higher Power. It doesn't matter what you call it as long as you learn to use it in your search.

The infinitely wise author Louise Hay reminds us that every time we say, "I don't know," we're shutting the doors to our inner wisdom. Your goal is to not block your spiritual knowing, and your inner career coach, but rather to listen. Many job searchers are beset by guilt when they take time to listen. They feel intense pressure to *do* something. Remind yourself that taking the time to listen *is* doing something. In fact, it may be the most important part of your job search.

Perhaps Michaelangelo said it best. When asked how he created the infamous statue of David, Michaelangelo remarked that he just chipped away at everything. You must likewise chip away at your long-held beliefs to discover the real truth inside of you.

Start by asking yourself what, for you, opens the dialogue with your inner voice. Quiet time? Running? Cleaning? Praying? Journaling? Gardening? Open the dialogue in whatever way works best for you, and then ask yourself these five questions:

- What's working well in your job?
- What isn't working?
- How do you want your work to be?
- What pieces of your job or past jobs do you want to take with you into your next job?
- What pieces do you want to let go?

In *Man's Search for Meaning*, the concentration camp survivor Victor Frankl writes:

> *Everyone has his own specific vocation or mission in life; everyone must carry out a concrete assignment that demands fulfillment. Therein he cannot be replaced, nor can his life be repeated. Thus everyone's task is unique as his specific opportunity to implement it.*

What is your "assignment?" What specific opportunities can you grasp to implement that mission?

Sometimes our inner coach is hard to hear over the din of others who, though well-meaning, are unfairly trying to shape our decisions based on their own needs or desires. If this is an issue for you, see Lesson 13.

Career Comfort:

My inner career coach guides me safely to my right path and mission. I open myself to the wisdom inside of me.

Let's Recap…

Leaving your job. That's a lot to think about. When you start to get overwhelmed, just remember that you are in control. It is your life, and your choice.

As you were working through the CONTEMPLATING lessons, did you find yourself creating barriers for yourself and trying to talk yourself out of leaving? We all do it. It simply means you have moved into the next phase of your journey. When you feel you are ready, I invite you to start the next set of lessons which will discuss those barriers and how to overcome them. And continue to hang on to the CAREER COMFORTS you've learned so far:

Career Comforts for Contemplating

Career Comfort:

Because I have a choice in what I believe, I am not stuck. I take care of myself, I have the freedom to make choices, and I have the ability to create the work life I want.

Career Comfort:

I bless this job and thank my Higher Power for sending it to me when I needed it. I am choosing to lovingly release it and pass it on to the next person who needs it. I now choose to move on to a position that meets my needs and helps me fulfill what is best in me.

Career Comfort:

People grow and change; if my job has not grown with me, I have the ability to choose a job that is right for me now.

Career Comfort:

I exercise my free will in my job search because I am in the best position to determine what is right for me.

Career Comfort:

I have options to consider other than leaving my job immediately.

Career Comfort:

I will know when I am ready and I will wait until then to take appropriate action.

Career Comfort:

I can trust what's right for me, and I can leave my job whenever the time is right for me.

Career Comfort:

I choose to say yes to all good, all opportunity, and all blessings. I choose to turn away from my own negativity and the negativity of others.

Career Comfort:

Listening to my pain will bring me to a new awareness of my values and aspirations. I have nothing to fear.

Career Comfort:

My inner career coach guides me safely to my right path and mission. I open myself to the wisdom inside of me.

Welcome to The OVERCOMING Lessons

I would argue that our most tenacious opponent in the job search is not a bad economy, the luck of the draw, or that well-qualified candidate vying for the same job we want. It is ourselves. We seem to do our very best to sabotage our own job search, and to talk ourselves out of what is clearly best for us. Why? Because we all have baggage: fear, self-doubt, pessimism and a host of unhealthy perceptions we've picked up along the way. Baggage creates barriers.

The good news is, we built those barriers, so we likewise have the power to tear them down. The following set of lessons is designed to guide you through the maze of barriers you may have created for yourself, and to help you knock them down one by one. This will not be easy. It will take hard work and commitment, and will require you in some instances to completely change your way of thinking. But you can do it.

The journey continues...

LESSON 11

Leave Your Job, Keep Your Friends

When I ask individuals who have recently separated from a job what they miss most, the most common response is "my coworkers." Often the most intense emotions in the grieving process center around leaving colleagues we've grown attached to, and knowing that the team will go on without us. We may even find ourselves missing those coworkers with whom we seemingly had little in common *but* our jobs. It's not unlike the bond that forms between soldiers in the same platoon; our coworkers become our brothers and sisters in arms on the front lines of the workplace.

Unfortunately, however, the anxiety we feel about leaving the platoon can cause us to stay in a job much longer than we should. It's not surprising that in *Keeping the Keepers*, a landmark study conducted by the National Association for Law Placement (NALP) Foundation on retention and attrition in law firms, a common reason cited by associates for staying at a particular firm was "the people."

The key to overcoming separation anxiety is two-fold. First, realize that the colleagues who have truly become an important part of your life will continue to be. You may not see them every day, but you can and should look for ways to continue to foster those relationships. For those of you contemplating starting a business or working as an independent contractor, it is not uncommon for your current employer or coworker to be either your first client or a key referral source.

Second, you may need to redefine your identity apart from the team. Accept that in order to grow professionally and personally, there comes a time when you need to spread your wings and test what you are capable of on your own, or as a member of a *new* team. Once you're in an environment where you no longer have your old, faithful comrades to fall back on, you'll most likely surprise yourself and find you have abilities you never knew you had.

EXERCISE

- List the coworkers with whom you truly want to continue a relationship after you leave your current job—what is it about each person that causes you to want to continue to have that person in your life?
- List ways that you might not just keep in touch with, but enhance your relationship with, each of those individuals.

Career Comfort:

I can choose to continue important relationships outside of the work environment, or reconfigure those relationships. I can redefine myself as an individual or as part of a new team.

LESSON 12

YOU ARE NOT YOUR JOB

IN THE PREVIOUS LESSON, WE TALKED about redefining oneself. Let's explore that further. It's not surprising that another barrier people encounter in a job change is the extent to which they have allowed their job to define their self-image. Western society has reinforced this concept for hundreds, if not thousands, of years. Many Anglo-European last names, for example, are derived from occupations. Smith, for example, refers to a "blacksmith"; Cooper means "barrel-maker." It persists today. When we're introduced to someone at a social event, one of the first things we're usually asked is, "What do you do for a living?"

The thought of leaving your job is overwhelming if the primary (or only) way you currently define yourself is, for example, as an accountant, or lawyer, or nurse. Realize that you are more than the sum and substance of your job. You have interests, relationships and a lifetime of experiences that have absolutely nothing to do with your current job, or any other job you've ever held. Focus on these aspects of yourself, and see yourself as a whole person, not only during a job transformation but at all times. It helps keep your job in perspective...especially on bad days.

Exercise

Write down five sentences that define you in the context of relationships, i.e., "I am the mother of three children," or, "I am John's closest friend."

Write down five sentences that define you in terms of your abilities (particularly those not closely associated with your current job), i.e., "I have a nice singing voice," or, "I am a good cook."

Write down five sentences that define you in terms of interests or hobbies you have, i.e., "I like to write poetry," or, "I know a great deal about the Civil War."

Write down five sentences that define your personal belief system or philosophies that are central to your life, i.e., "Environmental conversation is important to me," or, "I am a Christian (or Muslim, Jew, Pagan, etc)."

Career Comfort:

I am a multi-faceted person. With or without my current job, I will continue to be me.

LESSON 13

Turn Down the Volume of Others

Clients sometimes ask me how they'll know which voice is the "right voice," the real inner coach that you discovered in Lesson 10. My answer is that they'll know it by the sense of peace and joy that the voice gives them.

In my own case, even though I was leaving a lucrative job as a lawyer and taking the risk of starting a business, at my core I felt inner peace. The real challenge was turning off other people's voices and staying tuned to my own inner coach!

Ask yourself what part of your life gives you inner peace. Even if you find it in a hobby or in volunteer work, not in your work life, write it down. This is not the moment to be practical. Break it down even further: what aspects of that activity bring you that inner peace? If golf gives you inner peace, is it the social aspect? The competitive aspect? Being outside? If it's painting, is it the physical process? The creative outlet? The pride you feel in the end product?

The keys here are to listen to your own voice, not limit your search, and pay attention to what gives you peace and joy.

This can be difficult, especially if you are contemplating not just a change of employer, but a more drastic career change. Each of us has individuals in our lives—friends, parents, spouses—who feel invested in our careers. Maybe it's because they lent you the money to pay for your schooling, or stayed up late helping you study for exams. Maybe it's because your mom takes pride in telling her professional colleagues that her child is a dentist or a banker.

It always amazes me the lengths to which parental influence can control our lives, even when we are fully grown, successful, independent people. As a former practicing lawyer with what appeared to be a "great job" to everyone else but me, I know *I* can relate. One of my colleagues used to conduct alternative career seminars for lawyers contemplating leaving the profession. She would routinely ask audience members to raise their hands if one of the things holding them back was the fear that they would disappoint their parents. Without fail, almost every hand went up!

What you need to bear in mind is that no matter how invested others may feel and how well-meaning their advice may be, in the end there is only one person who has to get up every day and go do your job...and that is YOU. So YOURS is the voice that needs to rise above the others. One way to stay true to your inner career coach is to ask one person in your life to unconditionally support you in listening to your inner career coach. This needn't be (and often times isn't) your spouse, but rather someone who gets where you are at and why you are doing it. This can be a colleague, a friend, a counselor—again, listen to your inner career coach on that choice as well. For further discussions about finding that support person, see Lesson 28.

One final thought on the influence of others—you will find people ready and willing to give advice (and pass judgment) not only on the fact that you are job searching, but on *how* you go about that search. Some members of your support circle may insist that you must engage in a formal, structured goal-setting process or your search is doomed to fail. You'll find such formalized processes meticulously outlined in numerous self-help books, and advocated by many outplacement counselors and job-hunting support groups. If such a process resonates with you, that's great. But if "goal-setting" is a loaded word for you, or if the thought of setting down your goals to conform with a particular process or system makes job searching seem all the more daunting to you, then pay attention to your inner coach and take the approach that works for *you.*

One way you can do this is to think about your job search more globally. Ask yourself, "What do I want to manifest?" This kind of thinking helps you focus in on the "soul of the job," which is an important place for anyone to start, and may be the approach that works best for you. In short, there is no right or wrong way to conduct a job search, so feel free to ignore the well-meaning advice of others. Certainly, there are some tried and true activities that can prove effective in bringing almost any job search to fruition, such as networking (which is discussed in Lessons 33 and 34), but throughout your journey, if you do what feels natural to you, you will find that you do it with ease and grace.

Career Comfort:

I can trust my inner career coach—my job is to listen to it and to discern it from the voices of others.

LESSON 14

Loss Is a Signal We Are Alive and Growing

THERE'S A WISE OLD ADAGE THAT SAYS, "When one door closes, another opens." You must embrace that belief to your very core. As Julia Cameron reminds us in her book, *Blessings: Prayers and Declarations for a Heartful Life*, we can be comforted by knowing that the universe often blesses us by those very things that it procures from us either gently or not so gently.

Many of us are aware of loss and the need to let go in relationships, but not in our careers. We may be required, for instance, to let go of a job through downsizing or the sale of a company, or to let go of a title, a longed-for interview, a promotion, a co-worker, or a boss.

Letting go is difficult for many of us, because our western culture teaches us to "be someone" and above all to stay in control. Letting go, conversely, often demands that we *do* nothing, that we just *be*, without being *someone*. But letting go is a skill, and like any skill, it can be learned.

A key step in learning to let go is choosing to trust. Trust will pull you through your fear of loss and of the unknown. But learning how to trust means making a change in yourself. When I was at this stage in my transformation, the only way I could get to a place of trust was to make a *conscious decision* to trust. Even if I couldn't feel it, I had to decide to see things through trusting and faithful eyes. I had to decide that there was a better plan for my life—including my work life.

To do this, lean into your Higher Power and yourself. Learn to trust that the right job, the right promotion, the right opportunity is coming to you at the perfect time and in the right place. Trust that this is your chance to create your work life the way you want it to be. Trust that you deserve it!

And finally, when I'm helping clients create a better plan for their lives, I encourage them not to push away their feelings of loss. I'll tell you the same thing: your sense of loss tells you a lot about yourself. It contains important information about your reasons for needing change, and about your values and aspirations. If you embrace the loss and choose to learn from it, it will help you create your roadmap of change.

Exercise

- Describe the loss that you feel.
- What is your sense of loss telling you about your current work?
- What does it say about the job you'd like to have?
- What are you being asked to let go of?
- What pieces of your job do you want to take with you?

Career Comfort:

It's natural for me to feel a sense of loss. My way through the loss is through trust. I trust that the right job is coming to me now.

LESSON 15

TURN IT AROUND UNTIL IT WORKS

I LEARNED THE CONCEPT OF "TURN Arounds" from Gail Straub and David Gershon in their fabulous workshops, books and tapes on empowerment. It can be one of the most powerful and comforting tools in your job search toolbox.

In essence, turning something around means identifying the beliefs that limit you and then replacing them with beliefs that expand you. It's a mental process of flipping those self-imposed limits around and revamping them. It's about choosing to see things in a more empowering way.

We talked a lot in Lesson 8 about negative thoughts. Let's see how those can be turned around.

For example:

Limiting belief: All I know how to do is be a lawyer (sales person, teacher, assistant, nurse, etc.).

This is a belief we commonly impose on ourselves. But who created that belief? We did! So we can turn it around, can't we?

Turn-around: The only things holding me back are not knowing what else I can do with my background, and not having made the commitment to change. I can change those!

Limiting belief: I will never make this much money (have this much flexibility, work with such great people) anywhere else.

Turnaround: My Higher Power wants me to be prosperous and financially secure. The easiest way to wealth is to do the work I want and love.

EXERCISE

- What are your limiting beliefs about your work?
- Take each of those statements, and write the "turned around" version of it.
- What are your limiting beliefs about your right to success?
- Take each of those statements, and write the "turned around" version of it.

CAREER COMFORT:

I can easily turn around my limiting beliefs.

LESSON 16

What Color Are Your Handcuffs?

WE ARE ABOUT TO ENTER INTO A SERIES of three chapters on a topic that makes many of us uncomfortable, which is why we are going to spend some time on it and approach it from three different angles. I'm talking about money and what it means to us.

Let's start with your handcuffs. They may be the ubiquitous golden color, or they may be silver, bronze or even a slightly tarnished shade of pewter. Regardless of how brilliant their hue, it's become a cliché that what often holds us back from making a job change is the fear that we will have to change our lifestyle when we give up our present income. Let me start by telling you what this chapter is *not* about: nowhere in here will you find an admonishment to run to the nearest financial advisor, nor does it include a step-by-step worksheet on how to plan a budget. Because the truth is, until you have carefully examined those handcuffs, and determined not only what color they are but how they got there, you are in no position to even begin the process of financial planning.

So let's start first with some basic truths.

1. **You put the handcuffs on, and you can take them off if you want to.** Like so many other things we've talked about in this book, the income that you have and the income that you need are within *your* control. They are not the result of fate; they are not some condition that has been arbitrarily placed upon you. Just as you chose the job that pays you your current salary, you can likewise choose your next move. Granted, we all have some expenses that are more or less fixed, like the electric bill and student loans. Still, you have much more freedom than you think; it is merely a matter of choosing to exercise that freedom.
2. **You *can* live off less**. You are not going to starve to death if you take a pay cut, unless you are currently living at or below the poverty level. The World Bank reports that more than 2.7 billion human beings worldwide currently live off less than $2.00 a day. Clearly, our concept of what one "needs" to live is skewed as compared to the rest of the planet. Moreover, you've lived off less before. If your career has steadily progressed over the years, your present income is probably the largest you have ever experienced. Like many of us, you lived off rice and beans in college, and for some time thereafter. A colleague of mine recently shared with me that her first job out of college paid a whopping $12,500 per year. After rent, car insurance and taxes, she had exactly $98 a week left over. And it was the happiest time of her life. Many of us can relate.
3. **People will always spend more than they have, no matter how much they have.** It's a natural human tendency to live just slightly beyond our means no matter what our income. The colleague in the story above said when she was making $12,500, she was always a little

strapped for cash. And she would think to herself, "What must it be like to make $20,000 or $30,000 a year? If I could just make that much, I'd never be strapped for cash again." Then she went to law school. Upon graduation, her first job paid $54,000 a year, which was more money than she had ever imagined possible. And at that income level...she was always a little strapped for cash. The point is, our "needs" tend to keep up with and just slightly exceed our income—so it stands to reason that if our income level drops, our "needs" will eventually adjust downward as well.

4. **There is no "point of no return**." Let's say that you take the plunge and quit your current job in favor of one that makes you happier but pays substantially less. And let's say that after a year of this lifestyle, you find that your blissful state of self-actualization in the workplace simply does not outweigh your intense desire to purchase another pair of Manolo Blahnik shoes or Callaway clubs. Are you destined to spend the rest of your life dejectedly sulking past the display window of your favorite shoe or sporting goods store? No. You can always go back. Maybe not to the exact same job, but if you've had success in your industry to a point where you're wearing designer handcuffs, your slight career detour will not keep you out of the running for another, more lucrative job. It won't be long before you're back to buying Gucci handbags and lunching at your favorite restaurant. If that's what you really want, you can have it again. Think of your income decrease as an experiment, if it makes you feel better.

Hopefully by now the message has come through loud and clear that you are the one in control of how packed full of "all the stuff that money can buy" your life is. Just for fun, let's start to unpack your life. Make a list of all the things in life that make you happy. Really let your mind go; think expansively. Anything is fair game, i.e., the sound of your children laughing, the taste of your favorite ice cream (definitely "Chubby Hubby" for me), or driving down the road in your little red Corvette. Come up with a list of fifteen to twenty things.

Now look at your list. How many of the items are tangible goods, as opposed to people, activities or places? Of those tangible goods, how many of them cost more than $100? More than $1000?

Let's try another exercise. Make a list of ten items you currently own which you would consider to be luxury items. Of those items, which would you describe as something you *desperately* wanted—as opposed to something you bought just because you felt you deserved it, or felt it was something a person at your income level "should" own. Now of those items in the desperate category, how many of them turned out to be every bit as wonderful as you imagined they would be? How many of them continue to hold the same fascination for you today as they did the day you bought them? How many of them do you use on a daily basis? On a weekly basis?

What did you learn? Perhaps your answers revealed that you are not as wedded to the high-ticket items in your life as you have programmed yourself to think you are. If so, living at a lower income level in exchange for career satisfaction may not be a drastic change for you after all. Then again, maybe the exercises revealed that you are in fact pretty firmly entrenched in your current lifestyle. That doesn't mean you always will be, or that a career change is out of the question for you. It simply means it is going to require a more radical paradigm shift for you. Simply recognizing that is half the battle.

One final thought...more often than one might think, it's not so much the items that we can buy with the golden handcuffs that hold us back, as it is the *identity* that we derive from those handcuffs. We feel a sense of accomplishment being in a particular income bracket. We like being able to pick up the dinner tab when we go out with friends; we like being the one who always brings the most expensive gift to the birthday party. This is very much like the identity issues that surround our particular job title, which we discussed in Lesson 12. If you feel a substantial part of your identity is tied into your income level, I encourage you to go back to Lesson 12 and work through the exercises again.

Career Comfort:

How much money I truly need is based almost entirely on my own perceptions. I have the power to change my perceptions if I choose.

LESSON 17

MONEY IS THE EASY PART

WE'VE EXAMINED YOUR HANDCUFFS; now let's take it a step further. You have to learn to stop giving money so much power in your job search. I know that isn't easy. A European colleague of mine once commented on how we Americans are always talking about money—how much something costs, what a deal we got, etc. Money is a huge part of our culture, our belief system, and often our family structure. And on top of that, the bills always need to be paid. But if you learn how to conquer your money angst, you'll open up a whole new way of life.

Don't misunderstand me; I'm not saying you should be irresponsible during your career search. Taking care of the money aspect of our lives is critical. It is an act of self-love, and we need to honor that. What I'm talking about is taking a broader view by adopting a *prosperity mindset.* At its core, a prosperity mindset requires us to embrace the belief that there will always be enough money, success and opportunity to go around for everyone. This is not an easy mindset to acquire in our competitive society. In her book, *How to Turn Your Money Life Around: The Money*

Book for Women, Ruth Hayden reminds us that our money beliefs, like relationship beliefs, are often the result of our family systems and learned behavior.

To believe that money is the easy part, we have to consciously learn to push away our cynicism. This part didn't come easily to me at all. I had provided for myself since I was thirteen, and as a result, I constantly worried about money. I also had a whole set of unhealthy and unproductive beliefs about money such as, "money doesn't grow on trees," and, "money changes people." One day, Andy Ogren, one of my business mentors told me, "Pat, get over it. Money is the easy part." I looked at him blankly, thinking to myself, "Yeah, that's easy for you to say." (He is quite successful and I was living on rice and beans at the time.) But he was right. In time, I learned that I could spend my energy worrying about money or I could choose to spend it making myself successful. The choice was up to me. I chose to recognize that part of my journey was to learn a whole new set of beliefs, and to cultivate the belief that worrying about money accomplishes nothing and only drains my energy. That new belief didn't manifest overnight, but in time it came. And yes, I now firmly believe that money is the easy part.

So ask yourself if money is the piece that is holding you back in your job search. If so, choose to create a new set of beliefs for yourself by working through the following exercises.

Exercise

- What are your beliefs about money?
- Were you taught that money is your right?
- Were you taught, or did you choose to believe, that money doesn't grow on trees?
- Do you believe that money is evil or that too much of it will make you a bad person?
- What beliefs do you want to hold about money?
- Do you want to believe that making money is easy?

For more ways to put the money issue into perspective, continue on to Lesson 18.

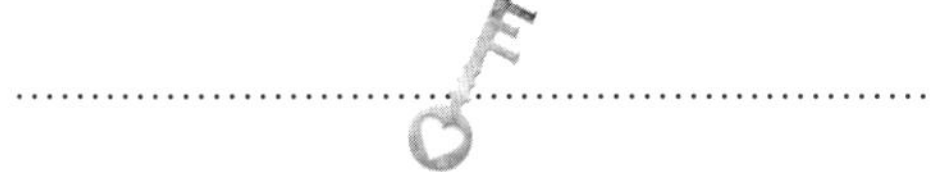

Career Comfort:

I choose to believe that prosperity is my right and comes to me easily.

LESSON 18

Prosperity Is More Than Money

In Lesson 17, we talked about how money is the easy part. That's because money is a merely an exchange of energy. We assign a lot more power and meaning to money than it deserves, and we usually confuse it with prosperity or abundance!

Prosperity is a much broader and more individualized concept than just money. It will have a different meaning for you than it does for me. That's because in the "exchange of energy" equation, I may place more emphasis on certain parts of the equation, while you focus on others. Consider these scenarios: 1) Your job pays well, but it requires you to put in a lot of hours, and those hours are not flexible; 2) You enjoy a high degree of flexibility, but you ultimately put in a lot of hours for relatively low pay; or 3) The pay stinks, but you work relatively few hours compared to most people you know and you have plenty of flexibility. If you take the exchange of energy view, each of those scenarios could leave you feeling prosperous, depending on which factors you weigh most heavily. The point is, your view will be different than mine.

Until you understand what prosperity means to you, chances are good that it will elude you. You'll continue to operate from a place where you think you should feel prosperous or you'll allow others to define it for you. Until you believe that you don't depend on other people, on a job or on external conditions (economic or otherwise), you lack prosperity thinking. Prosperity is self-defined.

On a related note, while you are redefining what prosperity means to you, don't limit yourself by assuming that your income can only come from one place. Many successful individuals now have shifted to earning their living from multiple sources. Your job is a source of income; it need not be your *sole* source of income. Think creatively. Are there ways besides your nine-to-five job that you could supplement your income? Do you have interests or talents that you could turn into a weekend, cottage industry? Would your area of expertise allow you to do some independent contracting or consulting on the side? Several of our clients now split their time between two different employers. The more options you open yourself up to, the more freedom you have to choose a job that you will really enjoy, without constantly thinking about the limiting money factor. There are no rules. Consciously move away from relationships and people who view prosperity one-dimensionally. Give yourself permission to think about all the ways you can be prosperous.

Exercise

- How do you define prosperity?
- Which factor is most important to you in the prosperity equation: salary, flexibility, or the number of hours you are expected to put in?
- Are there other factors that you can identify?

Career Comfort:

I determine what prosperity means to me, and I think creatively about how to achieve my definition of prosperity.

LESSON 19

ACCEPT—AND CONQUER!—ANXIETY

WE'VE WORKED THROUGH SOME OF THE anxiety surrounding money, but do you find that you're still feeling anxious about other aspects of making a change? Anxiety is a debilitating emotion and can keep you from landing in your right work. I've come to believe that much of the anxiety around a job change grows out of the identity crisis we experience when we're not working. So many of us identify ourselves so completely with our jobs that when the job is gone we feel lost—and anxious. We talked about this quite a bit in Lesson 12.

No matter how far we've come in learning to trust, we can't always get rid of anxiety. But we *can* keep it from paralyzing us. One way to do this is to utilize a "worry box." Take an empty shoebox and give yourself permission to worry as much as you want for a set amount of time—15 minutes or, if need be, one or two hours each day. During that time, write down what you're anxious about and place your worries in the box. When your worries bubble up outside of your worry time, gently remind yourself that this is not the time and that you can add new worries to the worry box the next day.

Another way to manage anxiety is to focus on the present moment rather than the past or the future. Learn to define yourself by what you do today, not by what you used to do. Of course, we all define ourselves by our backgrounds, but focus on the activities and associations you're presently engaged in.

That sounds simple, but it isn't! It can feel like you're abandoning your accomplishments. Remind yourself that you're not! You're redefining yourself, which is a very powerful thing.

You don't have to do this perfectly or all the time. Learn to do it some of the time, and be gentle with yourself. Congratulate yourself for the steps you make along the way.

Career Comfort:

I am safe and secure. No harm can come to me.
I am worthwhile and my right work comes to me
in the right place and at the right time.

LESSON 20

We Don't Fear All Change

LET'S TALK ABOUT A CONCEPT CLOSELY related to anxiety. The fear of change comes in many shapes and sizes during a job search. It manifests itself as a fear of leaving the devil you know for the devil you don't, as a fear of what others will say about you, and as a fear of what you're going to give up if you leave the job you hate.

It helps to remember that we don't fear *all* change. We aren't afraid of a new car, new clothes or winning the lottery. A job change, though, is often very different because it not only takes you out of your comfort zone, but can also bring up lots of unresolved stuff. It is amazing the lengths to which people will go to stay in a bad situation just because it's familiar. In the movie, *The Shawshank Redemption* (based on the novel by Stephen King), "Red" is released after many years in prison. But rather than reveling in his newfound freedom, he spends most of his waking moments thinking of ways to get back *in* to prison. As horrible as prison life was, he found he preferred the daily routine of it to the unpredictability of life on the outside. And so it is with us—we will endure a job we hate, rather than face the uncertainties of the job market or the untested waters of a new job.

In surpassing this, it is helpful to remember that your career fear is really the barrier between you and what you want. The formula for overcoming this barrier can be summarized in three words: Face, Embrace, and Overcome.

Step One: You must face, or acknowledge, your fear. That may be harder than you think, as we often try to fool ourselves or deny what's really going on. So take your time. Avoid clichés, and try to dig into what really lies at the heart of your personal fears. Ask yourself the following questions, and answer them honestly:

- If you were to name your fear, what would you call it?
- What would it look or sound like?
- What effects does this fear have on you?

Step Two: Once you've given your fear a name—its REAL name—it's time to embrace it by exploring it fully. A lot of fear comes from not knowing who and what we really are. In the context of a job search, our fear typically comes from not knowing what we want from our careers or what marketable skills we have to offer. Ask yourself:

- Where does this fear come from, or, what caused this fear to manifest itself?
- What you would choose to do if you were not afraid?
- What would you do if you were not afraid of the money part of job change?
- What aspects of a new job are you not afraid of? (more money, more status, increased responsibility, etc.)

Step Three: After you've acknowledged and explored your fear, overcome it. It boils down to one simple question:

- What is more important to you: avoiding your fear at all costs, or being true to yourself and getting what you really want?

Career transformation is about moving from self-improvement to self-actualization. Only once you have faced, embraced and overcome your career fears can you move to the next level.

CAREER COMFORT:

"We have nothing to fear
but fear itself."
—Franklin Delano Roosevelt

LESSON 21

YOUR GENDER IS SHOWING, PART 1

WE'VE TALKED ABOUT SOME OF THE self-imposed barriers that many of us share. Let's talk now about a few of them that seem to be somewhat gender-based. Though we've certainly come a long way, Baby, to this day perceptions about gender roles can affect your job search process. The sooner you recognize that and deal with it, the faster you can move ahead. If you are a woman (or want to learn more about the job search from a woman's perspective), read on. If you are of the testosterone persuasion (or just curious about how men's job search hang-ups differ from women's) see Lesson 22.

Differences between gender values in the workplace have been vigorously researched since World War II, when women first entered the work force in significant numbers. Though some of the studies reveal contradictory results, many researchers agree that there are substantial differences. According to social psychologist Satvir Singh,

> *Men tended to be more concerned about money, independence, security, and long-term career goals whereas women tended to*

> *be more people oriented, environmental oriented, and preoccupied with short-term career goals.*

From what I've observed in working with clients over the years, one of the most significant ways in which these differences manifest themselves is in the area of self-promotion. Women generally aren't as naturally inclined to self-promote as men are. That can really hamper one's job search, which is, after all, all about self-promotion. Socialization may be at fault, at least in part. Little girls are more likely to be told, "don't brag," and, "be humble and polite," while bragging and topping each other's stories are common forms of male bonding. I believe, however, it may be due even more to a fundamental difference in philosophies between men and women, and how they believe success is achieved. Most women believe that the way to get ahead is by doing a good job; if you work hard enough, the quality of your work will speak for itself, and someone will surely recognize it in time. Men, on the other hand, believe that doing a good job is a given. You get ahead by telling others you've done a good job. As a result, men are more likely to keep themselves open to opportunities, and to position themselves to seize those opportunities when they come along.

This is not an admonishment to become a shameless self-promoter; no one likes a braggart. But women can learn a great deal from their brothers in the work place. Start practicing now, in the job you are in, so that when the time comes to start a full-blown job search, or to seize an opportunity that has presented itself, it will feel natural. Take credit for your own work; it demonstrates self-esteem and confidence. If your team has accomplished something noteworthy, send out a memo or email telling other departments about it, and detailing how it will benefit them.

What may also be holding you back is the natural tendency many women have to underestimate their worth. If you suspect you may be doing this, it might be a good idea to take a look at Lesson 27.

Exercise

- List one or two accomplishments you have made in the workplace in the past several months.
- Who in your workplace should know about those accomplishments (i.e., your boss, your boss' boss, the management team, the entire staff, etc.)?
- As you look back on your performance reviews, what are some consistent themes demonstrating your aptitude?
- Describe effective ways you could communicate those accomplishments to those individuals or groups.

Career Comfort:

I recognize that job searching by its very nature involves promoting myself and my abilities, and I can learn to become comfortable with that.

LESSON 22

YOUR GENDER IS SHOWING, PART 2

WE JUST DISCUSSED THE SELF-IMPOSED barriers unique to women; now it's the men's turn. What holds men back in the job search process is often very different from what holds women back. Over the past four decades, the range of what society deems acceptable for women with respect to career choices has broadened significantly; a brief look around many neighborhoods finds roughly equal numbers of women who work outside the home, and those who choose to stay home.

Society has been much slower, however, to accept an expanded version of the male role. By and large, society still sees it as the man's role to be THE BREADWINNER and a good many men, even those who consider themselves enlightened thinkers on many other topics, internalize that. People often ask me who is happier in their jobs: men or women? My answer is always the same—for the most part there is no difference in satisfaction, but men just wait longer to give themselves permission to make a change. Typically it's when college is paid for and they've acquired a nest-egg. That's a long time to wait to be happy! If a man internalizes the perception that he should be responsible for the family's sole or primary income, and that he must earn a minimum amount, it can severely limit his thinking with respect to what jobs are available to him.

In Lesson 18, I advised all readers to think creatively about the money part. This is especially important if you are suffering from breadwinner syndrome. Think about whether your family really needs as much to live on as you currently believe it does. Have a heart-to-heart discussion with your partner; she may be willing and able to bear a larger part of the financial burden.

Societal views on "masculine" versus "feminine" professions also tend to prove more detrimental to men. Whereas a woman who ventures defiantly into a historically male-dominated profession like engineering might be dubbed a "pioneer" by family and friends, a man who leaves the construction industry to pursue a career in nursing might not receive the same admiring encouragement. Similarly, while a woman who makes a drastic career change is "brave" and a "risk-taker," a man contemplating such a change might be deemed "flaky" or "irresponsible" by those with pre-conceived notions about the role of a solid, upstanding breadwinner. These same lingering societal expectations may be why, while many organizations now offer some form of paternity leave, few men actually take it for fear that it stigmatize them and jeopardize their careers.

In short, my advice to male job seekers is the same I gave to all job seekers in Lesson 13. Turn down the volume of others—do not let others' limiting beliefs limit your own beliefs. And if you sense that you have internalized some of those limiting beliefs, turn them around until they work, as we discussed in Lesson 15. Life is too short to be bound by the expectations of others.

Career Comfort:

I decide what career is right for me based on my skills, abilities, and interests, as opposed to outdated societal norms. I do not have to bear the sole burden of providing for my family.

LESSON 23

Don't Walk—Run!—From Scarcity Thinking

WE'VE JUST JOURNEYED THROUGH SOME gender-based barriers. Now let's look at a barrier than affects all of us. The scarcity concept we are going to talk about overcoming in this lesson is in some ways related to, yet much broader than, the money issues we talked about earlier in Lessons 16–18. It has less to do with dollars and cents, and more to do with our beliefs about opportunity in general. Job searches are hard, so it's critical to surround yourself with people who operate from a sense of abundance, not scarcity.

The scarcity mindset is, unfortunately, everywhere. Just look at the language used in many want ads, and how people talk about looking for a job! You'll find an underlying tone of "not enough to go around," a sense that each possible job is the last job in the universe. But on a spiritual level, there is no competition. We have all been created differently and no two people will perform the same job in the same way.

Gently remind yourself that a scarcity mindset is a manifestation of fear—fear that there won't be enough jobs, enough money, enough abundance to go around. Remind yourself that this is an attitude that breeds unhealthy competition.

Rather than buying into the scarcity mindset and focusing on an imagined pool of candidates that exists outside of yourself, focus within. You can do this by building a strategy for how to communicate your talents and gifts to a prospective employer, and by trusting that the right employer will recognize your unique qualifications when the time is right.

Ask yourself what you have to offer the prospective employer. Everyone is gifted in many ways. What are your gifts? Don't just think about your *technical* skills here. Think about how you build relationships and relate to people. Does your gift lie in the way you deal with customers? The way you analyze a problem? Your work ethic? Your listening ability? Your ability to be a fair and trustworthy manager?

In *Emotional Intelligence: Why It Can Matter More Than IQ* and the follow-up, *Working With Emotional Intelligence*, management guru/author Daniel Goleman discusses how new discoveries in brain research prove that emotional stability is more important than IQ in determining an individual's success in life, and most notably, in the workplace. Even though employers don't often say so, emotional intelligence is one of the major factors that they look for when hiring. They almost always seek candidates who get along and communicate well with people at all levels of an organization. So think broadly about what your skills are and don't underestimate your ability to work well with all types of people.

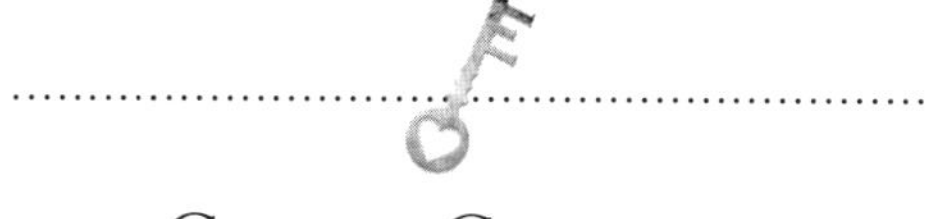

Career Comfort:

There is no need to compete because there is enough to go around. All I have to do is demonstrate my own gifts and talents, and how I would exercise them in my own unique way.

LESSON 24

Recovering from the "F" Word
OR
Being Terminated Is Not Terminal

WE'VE WORKED AT KNOCKING DOWN A lot of barriers so far! But what if you're thinking to yourself, "Pat, that's all well and good, but my barrier is unique. I didn't leave my job by choice." Call it whatever you like: fired, let go, laid off, downsized or terminated. The end result is the same. You won't be going back to your job. Now what?

First of all, realize that you will most likely go through the five stages of grief identified by Dr. Elisabeth Kubler-Ross in her groundbreaking book, *On Death and Dying.* These stages apply to *any* life-altering event that's difficult to accept, not just death. You will feel a succession of Denial, Anger, Bargaining, Depression, and finally, Acceptance. Acceptance is almost always last, but other than that, there are no set patterns for the order in which you will experience the other four stages, or how long each will last. Just know that you will experience them all, so be ready for them. Each stage is an essential step in your healing process, and only once you have experienced them all can you truly move ahead. Journal each stage, if you like, to keep track of where you are at in the process.

At every stage, I've found it helps my clients to fall back on one or more of the following tenets. Some are easier to internalize than others, depending on what stage you find yourself in at the moment (and pretty much all of these will tick you off during your Anger stage). But trust me—each of these tenets is true, even if you can't see it clearly right now.

1. **Things happen for a reason.** Yes, this departure from your job was not your choice—but that doesn't mean that in the overall scheme of things it's not a good thing. You've heard of blessings in disguise? I can't tell you how many clients have told me, after they've worked through the anger and shock, that being let go was the best thing that ever happened to them. It freed them from a job that, deep down, they really didn't like, and gave them the push they needed to move on to a better one. Which leads me to the next tenet...
2. **Use this time to your advantage.** Most of us don't take the time to really plan our careers until some major event—like being terminated—forces us to do so. You have been given the gift of free time. Use it to figure out what you really want to do, and where your strengths lie. You will probably never have another chance like this again.
3. **Being terminated is not a commentary on your worth as a human being.** There are many reasons why termination occurs that have nothing to do with you: office politics, corporate mergers, a poor economy, or the whim of some crazy HR manager hell-bent on restructuring your workplace to conform to the Strategic Plan du Jour. Worst-case scenario, you were let go because your particular performance on this particular job did not meet someone's particular expectations. Not because you're a bad person, not because you're stupid, and not because you're a loser. Remember Lesson 12 where we

talked about your identity apart from your job? Now might be a really good time to revisit that chapter, and focus on the non-work-related aspects of who you are.

4. **You can learn from this.** Let's say you were, in fact, terminated because of performance issues. Use that information as you move forward. Now you know exactly what is expected in the workplace. You will strive to improve upon your performance as you move into the next position. Life is a constant learning process; we make mistakes and we move on, learning from them as we go. Why should our work life be any different?
5. **Focus on the positive aspects of your job.** This one may take a while. For a long time, you will only be able to think of your former position as the job you got fired from. But in time, force yourself to look at all you got out of that job. Instead of thinking, "I got terminated by ABC Corporation," look at it as, "I was at ABC Corporation for 3 years; that's pretty good!" Make a list of all you learned in the job, the responsibilities you had, and the projects you completed. You'll find that even the most negative job experience has supplied you with skills you did not have before. Now build on them.
6. **You will find another job.** Termination is not a death sentence for your career. Many, many people are terminated, for a variety of reasons, and they go on to have successful, satisfying careers. If you don't believe it, take a look at Harvey Mackay's book, *We Got Fired!...And It's the Best Thing That Ever Happened to Us,* which profiles a number of well-known, successful individuals, all of whom were terminated at some point in their careers. It is not shocking for a prospective employer to learn that you did not leave your last job by choice, so long as you handle it effectively and appropriately in an interview setting.

Practice what you'll say; say it succinctly. Never badmouth your former employer, as tempting as it may be. And if you were terminated for performance reasons, tell your prospective employer what you've learned that will enable you to perform better going forward.

Here's a final word of advice to consider once you are ready to look for a new job: know what your former employer is going to say if contacted by a prospective employer. Many employers have a strict policy of confirming your employment dates, and nothing more. They will not comment on the circumstances of your departure. You should never lie in an interview, obviously, but it may not always be imperative for you to offer that you were terminated, depending on your former employer's policy. Some clients have even been able to negotiate a positive reference as part of their termination package. If it's not possible to get a positive reference from a former supervisor, see if you can line up references from a former coworker or someone whom you supervised. Someone who worked with you previously, and is now employed elsewhere, is often a particularly good choice, as they may be able to speak more freely.

Career Comfort:

I will use this time to rethink my career path. I will not allow myself to take this termination as a comment on my personal worth. I am thankful for what I have learned through this process, and I will apply it as I move ahead into my next job.

Let's Recap...

I TOLD YOU KNOCKING DOWN ALL THOSE barriers would be hard work! But with your new perspective and paradigm shift, you are ready to start the next phase of your journey. Congratulations! It's time to create a plan for your new life. The next set of lessons will help you do just that.

One final word of caution with respect to all the obstacles we've just worked through: unfortunately the work is not over and it never will be. Long-held negative beliefs die hard and can rear their ugly heads again down the road if we are not mindful of them. Continue to revisit the Career Comforts below as often as needed throughout the rest of your journey to avoid a "relapse."

Career Comforts for Overcoming

Career Comfort:

I can choose to continue important relationships outside of the work environment, or reconfigure those relationships.

I can redefine myself as an individual or as part of a new team.

Career Comfort:

I am a multi-faceted person. With or without my current job, I will continue to be me.

Career Comfort:

I can trust my inner career coach—my job is to listen to it and to discern it from the voices of others.

Career Comfort:

It's natural for me to feel a sense of loss. My way through the loss is through trust. I trust that the right job is coming to me now.

Career Comfort:

I can easily turn around my limiting beliefs.

Career Comfort:

How much money I truly need is based almost entirely on my own perceptions. I have the power to change my perceptions if I choose.

Career Comfort:

I choose to believe that prosperity is my right and comes to me easily.

Career Comfort:

I determine what prosperity means to me, and I think creatively about how to achieve my definition of prosperity.

Career Comfort:

I am safe and secure. No harm can come to me. I am worthwhile and my right work comes to me in the right place and at the right time.

Career Comfort:

"We have nothing to fear
but fear itself."
—Franklin Delano Roosevelt

Career Comfort:

I recognize that job searching by its very nature involves promoting myself and my abilities, and I can learn to become comfortable with that.

Career Comfort:

I decide what career is right for me based on my skills, abilities, and interests, as opposed to outdated societal norms. I do not have to bear the sole burden of providing for my family.

Career Comfort:

There is no need to compete because there is enough to go around. All I have to do is demonstrate my own gifts and talents, and how I would exercise them in my own unique way.

Career Comfort:

I will use this time to rethink my career path. I will not allow myself to take this termination as a comment on my personal worth. I am thankful for what I have learned through this process, and I will apply it as I move ahead into my next job.

Welcome to The PLANNING Lessons

YOU'VE MADE THE DECISION THAT YOUR job is no longer right for you, and that it is time to leave. You've made real progress in letting go of your baggage and knocking down the barriers to change. Now the real work begins. You know you want to go, but *where* do you want to go? Will you make a subtle change, or a radical one? What do you want out of your next job? This set of lessons will guide you through these questions, and will help you lay the groundwork for what lies ahead. If this is a journey, then the purpose of these lessons is to enable you to *fully envision* the destination that lies at the end of the road.

If you're like me and like to leaf briefly through a whole book before actually starting to read it, you may have noted that the "Planning" lessons comprise the shortest section of the book overall. Don't be fooled. They are every bit as crucial as anything else you will do on this journey, and will take as much or more time and hard work as anything you've done so far. You can't build a satisfying work life if you don't start with a solid, well-planned foundation. You can't get from Point A to Point B if you're not really sure where Point B is.

So let's get to work...

LESSON 25

DEFINE THE SOUL OF THE JOB

MY COLLEAGUE, GINA SAUER, IS FOND of saying that "90% of an effective job search goes on in your head; only 10% takes place in the outside world." What she means is that before you make a single networking call, respond to a single ad, or send out a single résumé, you must be very clear about what lies at the root of what you are looking for. I call it by a term originally coined by Gary Zukav: "the soul of the job." Having a firm handle on the soul of the job will determine the course of your search.

Defining the soul of the job is not as easy as it sounds. It is more than just the nature of the duties we perform. The soul of the job is what we hope to take from that job, at a very personal, spiritual level, and has a lot to do with the concept of self-actualization. It centers on how the job makes us feels about ourselves, and to what degree it allows us to do work that is consistent with who we really are. You may be saying, "But at the most basic level, doesn't everyone want the same thing from a job—to be paid fairly for work that satisfies them?" Basically, yes. But in defining what "satisfies them," people come to widely different answers. Figuring out what "satisfies" you will lead you to the soul of the job, and that discovery about yourself will keep you on track when you encounter distractions in your job search.

In Lesson 2, I shared with you how at the beginning of my own job search I wrote the following about the job I hoped to find:

> *I work with people who treat each other with respect. We recognize that blame and backstabbing drain our energy and creativity, and in no way serve our clients. My work allows me to express my creativity, learning, intelligence, and giftedness. I earn fantastic money easily, doing things that I love. My career is filled with abundance, intellectual stimulation and opportunity.*

What did I want to take from that job? A creative outlet. The freedom to exercise my intelligence and my gifts. A healthy paycheck with an emphasis on balance. The chance to prove myself. That's what satisfied me. You most likely want to take very different things from your job at a spiritual level.

Too often when we are contemplating a job change, we rush to try to figure out very specific details: what is the title of the job I want, what is its job description, what company do I want to work for? In a thorough, honest job search, however, these really are the minutia. The real meat of a job search, the part that can truly change your life, is the part where you ask yourself who you are and what you want. Only when you focus on the BIG questions first, will you go down a path that leads to the right job title, job description and employer.

Exercise

- What words describe you and your values at a basic, spiritual, personal level?
- What words describe the soul of your current job?
- Which of your values and passions does your current job speak to?
- Which of your core needs does it fulfill?
- Which ones doesn't it fulfill?

Career Comfort:

Throughout my job transition, I will remain clearly focused on the soul of the job I am seeking and I will let it determine my path.

LESSON 26

WORK IS NOT THE OPPOSITE OF FUN

A CRUCIAL STEP IN ENVISIONING YOUR destination is giving yourself permission to experience real joy in your next job. Maybe it was caused by one too many Dilbert® cartoons, but somewhere along the way most of us internalized the notion that work is not something to be enjoyed, but something to be endured. When was the last time you heard someone say, "I love my job"? After all, if it was fun, they wouldn't be paying you for it, right?

Wrong.

It's time to let go of that way of thinking. While I'm not so naïve as to suggest that you should love every single task that is ever assigned to you, or that you will spring out of bed singing every day when the alarm goes off, you can and should find something that brings you a real sense of satisfaction. And yes, even have fun. There may be a touch of martyr syndrome at work here; just as we believe that medicine has to taste bad to be good for you, we likewise succumb to the ridiculous notion that the only job worth doing is one in which we grit our teeth and dig in. In fact, the opposite is true—the happier you are in your job, the more productive you will be. If you find yourself gritting your teeth more often than smiling at work, it's a sign that you are probably not in the right place.

Self-doubt and issues of self-worth may be at play as well. We'll talk more about that issue in the next lesson. For now, remind yourself that you *deserve* to have a job that makes you happy.

The key to overcoming "work is by definition the opposite of fun" thinking, is to give yourself permission to be happy. We choose friends that we enjoy being around, we choose life partners who make us feel good, we choose vacation destinations based on where we think we'll have the best time, and we choose the house that has the most positive vibe. Why should our choice of job be based on any other criteria?

Exercise

- What makes you feel happy?
- Is it possible to experience any of those things in a workplace? Why or why not?
- Describe the places and times when you feel the happiest.
- What is it about those particular places/times that makes you happy?

Now take a moment to think about how it might be possible to recreate some of those scenarios/activities at work. For example, maybe you responded that you are happiest at the library, and what makes you happy about the library is that you get to read about topics that expand your thinking. Would it be possible to incorporate more intellectual challenge into your job and "expand your thinking" at work? Is there another job out there that provides you with greater intellectual challenge?

Career Comfort:

I take ownership of my happiness, and I look for a work life that will allow me to experience some of the same happiness in the workplace that I experience in other areas of my life. I give myself permission to enjoy my work.

LESSON 27

We're Only as Good as We Think We Are

You will not be able to envision the job that is truly right for you if you are limiting that vision based upon your own self-doubt. One of my saddest yet most eye-opening days as a headhunter was the day a client turned down a new position that paid twice her current salary because, as she put it, she "wasn't worth it." She loved the job she'd been offered, the boss and the company's location. She simply didn't believe she deserved it.

Until we do the inner work necessary to believe at our core that we are worthy of receiving our right work, it will elude us. We will continue to find ourselves in work that fails to maximize our giftedness and spirit.

In order to conquer self-doubt, we must recognize where it comes from. Often, feelings of insecurity about professional qualifications spill over from other parts of our life. A colleague of mine once counseled an individual who had a dazzling résumé; her background was tailor-made for the job for which she was applying. My colleague was amazed, however, at this candidate's lack of confidence...until the candidate revealed that she had recently been through a particularly difficult divorce that had drained her of self-esteem, including any self-esteem that might pertain to her job search. If you suspect something similar may be at play in your own job search, force yourself to step back with objective eyes. Pretend you are a prospective employer hiring for a job with a specific, defined set of criteria. Look at your résumé and objectively analyze it within the parameters of those criteria. How does it measure up?

This notion that we are only as good as we think we are may seem like fluff. However, in his book, *Mindful Loving*, and in his popular tape series, *The New Physics of Love*, the esteemed New York psychologist Henry Grayson asserts that a new science of relationships is dawning. That science reveals that behavior stemming from our own thoughts may manifest in the people around us. In essence, relationships succeed or fail according to how we think about them. So, if our relationships are, in fact, affected by how we view them, doesn't it follow that our relationship with ourselves manifests in others around us? Lack of confidence in ourselves not only keeps us from finding our right work, but makes us particularly susceptible to making the mistake of accepting a counteroffer. To avoid this pitfall, be sure to read Lesson 45 when the time comes.

Exercise

- What do you believe about your worth?
- Where does this belief come from? Point to specific examples of events or people that have shaped your beliefs about this.
- What do you believe about what you have to offer an employer?
- Look at your résumé. Write down three qualifications, skills or experiences that you have to offer an employer.

Career Comfort:

I deserve to have the jobs that I am applying for; I am qualified and ready to make my own unique contribution.

LESSON 28

FIND SOMEONE TO LEAN ON

AS ANY CAREER COUNSELOR WILL TELL you, a job change will put stress on you and your relationships. The partner or spouse of a job seeker goes through many of the same stresses as the seeker does, including all the worry about money and the anxiety of not knowing what the outcome will be. In addition, the spouse or partner is likely to feel the frustrations of a helpless bystander, excluded from much of the process.

While you're laying the groundwork for your change, it is incredibly helpful to pick one person in your network on whom you can unconditionally lean. This person should be someone who won't question your need for change and won't judge you for your choices. For some people, that person is a sibling or best friend; for others, it's a professional outplacement counselor. If you can, find someone who's been through a job change him or herself. With rare exceptions, it's my advice that this individual should not be your spouse or partner. That individual is under enough stress already! He or she may also be less than objective about what is truly best for you, because they feel they have a stake in your decision.

Clearly, however, your partner is a big part of your life and your support network. He or she needs to be involved at some level. The way to manage that is to make some clear up-front agreements with your partner. The contents of those agreements will vary depending on your unique circumstances. For many of my clients, simply agreeing that they will keep their partner informed can minimize lots of stress; when you make such an agreement, you don't have worry about getting asked about the progress and your partner doesn't have to constantly broach the subject with you.

Your agreement with your partner may also, for example, set financial or geographic parameters, or timelines. If you know you and your partner are going to be incurring some substantial, unavoidable expenses in the future, perhaps you can agree to take a job that pays no less than a minimum amount. If your partner is frustrated that your job search process has been taking longer than anticipated, perhaps you can commit to meeting certain benchmarks by an agreed-upon deadline. Or perhaps you'll agree to conduct your job search only within a certain radius of your current home, or in particular cities you both would consider living in. Whatever you and your partner agree on, it will go a long way toward making him or her feel more comfortable with, and supportive of, your career journey.

You may find that for you, the best person to lean on is a group of people, as in a more formal support group that meets regularly. Choose your group carefully, if you decide to go that direction. Some groups are very structured; each meeting follows a set outline, features specific weekly topics, and requires participants to do homework assignments. Others are more loosely structured, allowing participants to simply share whatever is on their mind at the time. While either may prove to be the right fit for you, one word of caution: the more loosely structured groups can, depending on the mix of individuals in the group, sometimes degenerate into "whining sessions" where participants seek to out-do each other with tales of woe and vie for the title of "Most Unfairly Treated." Such a group will do nothing to energize your job search and is, in fact, more likely to drag you down. For a refresher course on how to avoid negative thinking throughout your career journey, revisit Lesson 8.

Exercise

As you are identifying your career support person, ask yourself:

- Whom could you lean on unconditionally?
- How often will you check in with that person about your job search?
- At what specific time will you do that, and through what medium (phone calls, e-mails, lunch meetings, coffee breaks)?
- What information will you share and not share?
- How will you communicate some of the disappointments you encounter, and how can this person support you through those disappointments?

Career Comfort:

I don't need to do this alone, nor should I.

LESSON 29

Think In Terms of a Change Spectrum

IS YOUR VISION OF YOUR JOB DESTINATION becoming clearer? Do you see a small change or a big change at the end of the road? It's a basic tenet of economics that the biggest risks often reap the biggest rewards. And so it is with a job change. There are many types of job changes; some make for fairly smooth transitions, while others require us to do a 180° turnaround.

Think about throwing a stone into a pond and watching the ripples that form around the stone's point of entry. Imagine your current job is the point where the stone hits the water. The ring closest to it represents the more minor job changes—the ones most people can easily accept. You're a CPA working for a big accounting firm, for example, and you go to work for another big accounting firm. The next ring out represents those in which you're still doing the same type of job, but the environment changes. You're a CPA working for a big accounting firm, and you give up your lucrative salary to work at a smaller firm because you want a slower pace. That one might make some of your colleagues scratch their heads a bit more. The third ring out represents more drastic job changes, but ones which still arguably utilize your training and/or involve industries tangential to the one you're in. You're the same CPA as above, but you leave the big accounting firm to become the financial advisor to a newly formed venture capital company. Finally, there's the faint ring way at the edge of the pond. This time the CPA decides to become a ballerina. That's when your friends and family start to question your sanity...and you question your own.

People hesitate to make the big changes for three understandable reasons. One of the biggest hurdles is the push-back we get from friends, family and colleagues who can't understand why we would want to switch gears so radically and "throw away" our years of experience and our education. The more drastic the change, the more incredulous their responses, and the less support they might offer. It can be a scary proposition to embark on a job search without much support from your inner circle. This hurdle can be overcome, however. As I advised in the previous lesson, certainly there is someone on whom you can lean. If family and friends aren't offering much support, consider a job seekers' support group or an outplacement counselor. Once you've identified someone, it's much easier to turn down the noise of the naysayers, and listen to your own inner voice, as we explored in Lessons 10 and 13.

Another hurdle is that the less your new aspiration has in common with your current job, the more challenging it is to accurately judge whether it's the right fit. If your job change involves moving from a big CPA firm to a smaller one, while you can never be 100% certain that the new work environment will be well suited to your personality, at least you have a fairly firm grasp on the substance of the work you will be doing. If you plan to leave the CPA firm to pursue your dreams of becoming a ballerina, however, there are suddenly a whole lot more question marks. Not just the work environment will change, but so will the nature of your duties, the skills sets you will utilize, and the very "soul of the job." You have less direct access to information about your new aspiration; there's much more guesswork involved, making it much riskier. This hurdle, however, can also be overcome. Do whatever you can to take away as many question marks as possible before you make your final decision. Are there ways to ease into your new aspiration and test the waters before jumping in feet first? The CPA in our example could take a leave of absence from her CPA job to go to a month-long intensive ballerina camp. Or she could join an amateur dance company that rehearses only on weekends and doesn't interfere with her job. Gathering information that helps you assess whether a move is right is always crucial; it becomes twice as crucial when the contemplated move is a radical one.

The final hurdle is a practical one. It's relatively easy to network if you are looking for a job in your current industry. You have a ready-made list of colleagues you can start with. It's more difficult, however, when you are trying to break into an industry as an outsider. This hurdle, like the others, is not insurmountable; it just requires a little extra work. The same networking rules that we will discuss extensively in Lesson 34 apply. If you don't have a ready-made list of contacts, start identifying them. Read industry journals, join professional organizations, attend training seminars, surf the Internet and read everything you can about the movers and shakers in that industry.

Just remember: the fact that you trained for years for a particular profession, or that you have years of experience in your current field, are not in and of themselves reasons for staying in a similar or even tangential position. It's sort of like the old adage of "throwing good money after bad." If you have experienced several years of dissatisfaction, why would you want to stay on the same track in the same industry...and continue to experience more years of dissatisfaction? Know when to say "enough is enough."

Exercise

- Picture the job you want in relation to the job you are currently in. Is it a "close ripple" to your current job, or is it further out?
- What unique hurdles does that create in your job change process?
- How can you overcome those hurdles?

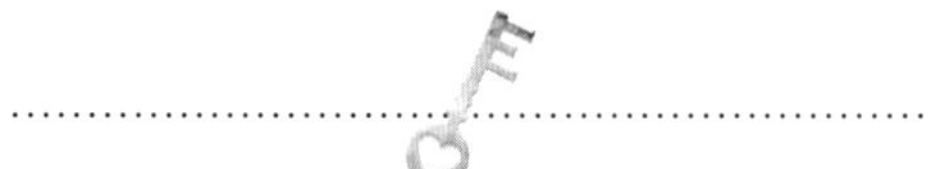

Career Comfort:

I have the power to reinvent myself. I understand that more radical job change brings with it more risks, but I am ready to face those risks, knowing that they can reap great rewards.

LESSON 30

Too Much School Isn't Cool

IF YOU THINK YOU MAY BE SUFFERING from what I call Perpetual Student Syndrome (PSS), read on. Note that it is possible to suffer from PSS even if you are not currently in school. PSS may be at work anytime we fail to pursue a job opportunity with the excuse that we need more credentials first.

In Lesson 38, we'll look at the kinds of feedback you might get once you are heavily into the "doing" phase of your search and are actually applying for jobs. Sometimes feedback is telling you that you need additional training before you are qualified for a particular position. If that is truly the case, and if you truly want that job, then by all means consider getting the training—after you have thoroughly weighed whether the additional time, energy and money it will cost you is reasonably calculated to reap the benefits you are hoping for.

Too often, however, individuals get locked in a pattern of seeking degree after degree, or getting one certification after another. The "Education" section of their résumé is pages long, while the "Work Experience" category remains woefully empty. While certain educational requirements clearly accompany certain careers—you can't practice law without a *Juris Doctorate* degree, and it's advantageous to be a CPA for many accounting positions—at some point you need to stop and ask yourself, how much is enough? As noted in an article on itworld.com, "Your goal should be to qualify for a job, not gain a paper credential that you can't back up with hands-on abilities." This perspective is not unique to the technology field. Most employers will tell you that they are far more impressed with seeing a job on your résumé that demonstrates your skills and abilities, as opposed to another Masters degree.

You also need to ask yourself what has kept you in school all this time. Love of learning? A genuine need to obtain certain educational requirements before you are prepared for your chosen field? Or is it possibly fear of getting out there into the real world—fear of rejection, fear that you won't be able to perform in a job, fear of the unknown?

Schools and other learning environments are generally very secure places because we know what is expected of us there. We are fed specific pieces of knowledge, which we are then asked to regurgitate in the form of a test, paper or project. But while our ability to think may be tested, our ability to *do*—and to do with a level of proficiency that would deserve a paycheck—really isn't. Some will argue that there is such a thing as "knowledge for knowledge sake." But for most of us, the reason we gain knowledge is so that we can actually apply it, and use it to move ourselves forward in life. In Lesson 11 we discussed how we all have to leave the "platoon" of our co-workers sometime. Likewise, at some point we all need to leave the sheltering arms of the ivy-covered walls.

Career Comfort:

I will not use education as a haven from the real world. I am ready to go out into the workplace and test the skills I have been trained to use.

LESSON 31

DON'T TAKE DEPRESSION LIGHTLY

IT'S GOING TO BE DIFFICULT FOR YOU TO fully realize your career vision if you are battling with depression issues. Let me say at the outset that I am not trained as a psychologist or psychiatrist, and if you suspect you may be dealing with depression, please seek the assistance of someone who is. My perspective on depression is limited to its hindering effect on your job search journey.

People use the word "depression" casually. Too often, depression is confused with sadness. But if you or someone you care about has ever experienced real depression, you know it's nothing to be casual about, and it's a whole lot more than being sad. According to the National Foundation for Depressive Illness, 15% of all self-inflicted deaths are attributable to depression. The World Health Organization has said that by 2020, depression will become the second leading health threat next to heart disease. It is further estimated by the National Institute of Mental Health that more than 80 million Americans—about 28% of the U.S. total population—suffer from a mental or attention disorder. Of this group, only about 20% will visit a doctor.

Prospective employers can pick up on depression in the interview process, and for this if for no other reason, you need to take it seriously. Some of the signs of clinical depression include: fatigue, insomnia, hopelessness, weight loss or weight gain, and feelings of helplessness. If you have these symptoms, it is important to be tested for depression and take extra steps to care for yourself in the job search process.

Many of our clients report that when they're depressed it's next to impossible for them to access their inner career coach. As such, until the depression lifts, you may not be in an appropriate place to be making career decisions.

Whether you choose to take anti-depressants or herbal treatments or seek other forms of treatment is up to you, but in my experience clients who have sought help show a remarkable change in their ability to cope with the job search. I'm constantly amazed at the number of highly successful people who struggle with depression. So don't see depression as a failure or weakness on your part; in fact, acknowledge that it takes courage to get help and congratulate yourself for taking that step.

If you do suffer from depression, view this as an opportunity to learn a new set of work and life skills. You may have been beating yourself up for a long time; this is a chance to stop doing that.

Career Comfort:

I will take care of myself and get help if I need it. Only then can I truly move forward.

Let's Recap...

Now you're really getting somewhere! You have a much clearer vision of where you are going. You are finally ready to start the active process of getting from point A to point B. The next and final set of lessons will take you through those essential steps, both the practical and the spiritual.

Just remember: if you are truly going to achieve your goal of finding the right job, you must remain true to the vision that you created for yourself in working through this last set of lessons, and you must constantly compare the opportunities that come your way to the criteria you have set. Turning back to the Career Comforts you've just internalized will help you do so.

Career Comforts for Planning

Career Comfort:

Throughout my job transition, I will remain clearly focused on the soul of the job I am seeking and I will let it determine my path.

Career Comfort:

I take ownership of my happiness, and I look for a work life that will allow me to experience some of the same happiness in the workplace that I experience in other areas of my life. I give myself permission to enjoy my work.

Career Comfort:

I deserve to have the jobs that I am applying for; I am qualified and ready to make my own unique contribution.

Career Comfort:

I don't need to do this alone, nor should I.

Career Comfort:

I have the power to reinvent myself. I understand that more radical job change brings with it more risks, but I am ready to face those risks, knowing that they can reap great rewards.

Career Comfort:

I will not use education as a haven from the real world. I am ready to go out into the workplace and test the skills I have been trained to use.

Career Comfort:

I will take care of myself and get help if I need it. Only then can I truly move forward.

Welcome to The DOING Lessons

YES, IT IS FINALLY TIME TO *DO*: TIME TO network, write cover letters and résumés, go out on interviews, compare offers and negotiate the best arrangement for yourself. But don't let the name of this set of chapters fool you. In this final phase, there is still plenty of contemplating and introspection left! This set of lessons will take you tell you how to do all the "nuts and bolts" of your job search more effectively, but it will also continuously challenge you to stay true to yourself, to conquer bad habits, and to fight the obstacles you place in your own path. It will also buoy your spirits when your job search is not progressing as quickly as you'd like, or in quite the manner that you'd hoped. You've come so far already. It's time now for that last big burst of effort and energy.

The end of your journey is in sight...

LESSON 32

WRITE YOUR PROPOSAL RIGHT

REMEMBER WAY BACK IN LESSON 5 where we discussed how staying at your job might be an option if you could make some meaningful changes and redefine your job duties?

Perhaps at this point on your journey, after much soul-searching and earnest investigation of your options, you've decided that what makes the most sense for you is not to leave your job but to re-sculpt it. You've convinced *yourself*; now you need to convince your *employer.*

Unfortunately, your employer is not motivated by the same things you are; your self-actualization is not a compelling factor for her. Moreover, your employer does not want to have to put much thought or effort into your job re-sculpture. You need to recognize that it is your job to make the case for change, and to do as much of the work for her as possible. In essence you are writing a business plan and need to put your "business hat" on.

The specifics and formality of your proposal will obviously vary depending on your job title and industry, but the following basic components should be part of almost any re-sculpting proposal:

1. **Summary section outlining reasons for change.** This needs to grab your employer's attention. State succinctly what kind of change you are proposing and make a list of justifications for the change. Why does your proposal make sense for your department and the company as a whole? What reasons have led you to request this change? Are certain aspects of your job no longer essential? Could they be more efficiently performed by others? Why? Do you have too much on your plate? Are some of your duties better aligned to the goals and duties of other departments? Would you be able to contribute more by focusing on particular aspects of your job? Remember, that although simply keeping you as an employee may be a motivating factor for your employer, you'll have more success if the justifications you offer show demonstrate widespread benefits.
2. **Current and proposed job descriptions.** Summarize what portions of your job you propose you will keep and which will be re-assigned or done away with. Attach an "official" copy of your current job description from the HR department. Draft a proposed job description based upon that model, and spell out how the old job description and the new differ. (You will get HUGE points for this, as it will save the HR department a lot of hours!)
3. **Reassignment of Duties.** You need to spell out the succession plan in detail. Who will take over the duties that you are leaving behind? Why does

that make sense? How will it impact your department, and other departments? The goal here is to convince your employer that the change will not have a negative impact on anyone; you are not simply "dumping" your undesirable duties. Rather, the realignment makes sense from a strategic standpoint.

4. **Resources.** Employers are more likely to approve a change if it doesn't cost them anything, or if the up-front costs are reasonably calculated to be offset or exceeded by overall savings in the end. Think about what you will need to make your proposed change happen. Will you need additional support staff or upgraded technology? A travel allowance? A marketing budget? Then get out your calculator and show how the new strategy will ultimately make your company money or cut costs. As always, money talks.
5. **Transition Plan.** Even if your employer thinks it all sounds good so far, she is still going to be apprehensive about how this is going to play out. What steps will your department and others have to go through to make this a reality? Spell it out, in detail. Shoulder as much of the burden as possible. Offer to train anyone who is taking on duties that used to be yours; offer to get any additional training you need on your own dime and on your own time. The transition should require as little time and effort as possible in order to be persuasive. Be sure to include a realistic timeline for the transition and what your anticipated results will be.

Job sculpting *does* work, and employers today are more likely than ever to recognize that re-sculpting a job is almost always preferable to losing a valuable employee and having to hire and retrain their replacement. You can go a long way toward making your re-sculpting goal a reality with a well-thought out proposal that covers all the bases.

Career Comfort:

I will write a job sculpting proposal that meets my goals and makes sense for my employer. I recognize that I have to take the lead in making the re-sculpting happen.

LESSON 33

STOP MAKING EXCUSES AND START NETWORKING

MAYBE THE LAST LESSON LEFT YOU saying, "Forget about proposing changes in my current job; I'm really ready to leave!" Networking is one of the keys to a successful career change, yet many of us are just terrified of it. We allow our misconceptions about it create barriers for us. When we look inside ourselves to discover what's behind our hesitation, what we often find is fear of rejection, shyness or uncertainty about how to begin. Even if you aren't completing an immediate job change, networking is a life skill that all of us should make better use of in every phase of our work and non-work life.

Many of us fall into the trap of thinking that networking is a huge time commitment that really doesn't get us anywhere. Often, what really hangs us up is the sense that networking is synonymous with imposing on people. As with most things, however, it's all in the way you look at it. How you view networking will determine what networking is for you. If you think it means bugging your friends and colleagues, then it will be. If, on the other hand, you see it as an opportunity to uncover new types of jobs, explore new ideas and meet new people, then that's what it will become for you.

The way around the networking challenge is to adopt a mindset that sees networking as a way to build relationships and perhaps more importantly, give back to those relationships. See it as an opportunity for you to give as well as get. This will go a long way toward dispelling your concerns that you are "using" others.

If that doesn't do the trick, consider this: networking is, in essence, merely asking people to share information. When your car breaks down, do you feel you are imposing on someone by asking them to refer you to a good mechanic? Of course not. So why is asking them to refer you to someone who may know about a job opportunity any different? Moreover, remember that people like to talk about things they feel they are knowledgeable about; asking them to share information often gives them a sense of pride and makes them feel useful. It allows them the opportunity to "give back" for all the times when they were in your shoes and someone helped *them*.

And don't allow yourself to use the excuse that no one in your circle of friends is terribly influential or important, or in a position to get you a job. When you think about networking, you need to think in terms of not just friends, but acquaintances and people you *hope* to meet. In fact, the odds are that an acquaintance, and not a friend, will be the person most likely to connect you with a job opportunity. In the book *Six Degrees: The Science of a Connected Age*, author Duncan Watts discusses the "weak tie" theory first introduced by sociologist Mark Granovetter. In the arena of job hunting:

> *...it is not your close friends who are of most use to you. Because they know many of the same people*

> *you do, and may often be exposed to similar information, they are rarely the ones who can help you leap into a new environment, no matter how much they want to. Instead it tends to be casual acquaintances who are the useful ones because they can give you information you would never otherwise have received.*

So with those objections to networking out of the way, it's time to work on overcoming the obstacles of shyness and fear of rejection. Before you head down the networking road you must accept that a certain percentage of people *will* tell you they are not in a position to help you, or they'll simply fail to return your phone calls (which is just a less direct of saying the same thing!). Do not take it personally; it is not a reflection on you. It simply means that they do not have the information you need. If that's the case, thank them anyway and, if appropriate, offer to share with them down the road what you learned or at least how you get there. Be buoyed by the knowledge that for every non-responsive individual you encounter, there will most likely be at least five others who empathize with your search process and will do what they can to help.

One of the most common objections I hear about networking is that often it doesn't feel like we are *doing* anything. After all, isn't networking just *talking* to people? Networking isn't as easily quantifiable as, for example, mailing out résumés or answering want ads. There's a certain amount of satisfaction in being able to say, "I mailed out 562 résumés last month!" But that is not how the majority of jobs are found. According to studies by the U.S. Department of Labor as well as Harvard University, approximately two-thirds of all new jobs are found through networking. Many employers will tell you that the jobs that are posted often pull in hundreds of résumés in response. Moreover, as a headhunter I hear over and over from employers that in assessing future employees, the candidate's attitude is a key factor. In short, in the end you will probably get more bang for your buck from a meaningful, twenty-minute phone conversation, even if the reward is not immediate, than from sending out myriad unsolicited résumés.

And don't fall into the Technology Trap! In the past years, I have heard more and more excuses from clients that they shouldn't have to network because "all job hunting is done on the Internet nowadays anyway." Wrong! It is certainly true that the Internet can be a very useful tool to research potential employers, and many of those employers now prefer to, or even exclusively, accept applications online. There are entire books written on how to conduct an Internet job search, and even the most technologically challenged among us can perform a simple online search that uncovers countless job-hunting web sites. But think about it: hundreds of people apply for jobs posted in the paper. With millions of people logging onto the Internet daily, the competition for jobs posted there is even more intense.

Moreover, I remain convinced that no matter how technologically "advanced" our society becomes, the real life connections we make with people will always be our number one source for jobs, and human beings will always prefer to hire someone they have met face to face, or who have been referred by someone they know, as opposed to hiring someone with whom they have no connection beyond an application on a computer screen. In short, technology is just another tool in your arsenal; it is not an excuse to be lax in your networking.

Finally, if what's holding you back from networking is utter confusion over where to begin, you need a game plan.

The next chapter will help you with that. Put one foot in front of the other, and read the next lesson to unlock the secrets of effective networking.

Career Comfort:

Networking is what I make of it; I determine whether or not it's an imposition on others by the way I choose to go about it.

LESSON 34

It's All About Relationships

NOW THAT YOU'VE OVERCOME YOUR emotional reservations about networking, you're asking, "OK, but *what* do I do?" Unfortunately, networking has been turned into a big, mystical concept (not unlike the perfect golf swing, for you fellow golfers!). It's actually quite basic.

In 1967, Stanley Milgram hypothesized in his now-famous study, "The Small World Problem," that every person in the United States is connected to every other person in the United States by a chain of no more than six people. His hypothesis was recently confirmed in an experiment using e-mail conducted by the author/sociologist Duncan Watts and his colleagues. Think about it. If these learned scholars are right, then it stands to reason that your dream job is just six people or less away! Thus your goal in networking is to uncover the connections you need and make them grow.

Start with a list of the people you know. Categorize them into rough groups: Work-Related, Social Acquaintances, Close Friends, etc.

Ask yourself these questions about each person:

- How do I know this person?
- What do we have in common?
- What types of people could this person introduce me to?
- What do I bring to this person, and how can I be of use to him or her?
- How can I foster this connection?

Remember too, that the best way to discover new people who might have helpful information to share with you is to go to those places where such individuals are likely to congregate: meetings or other events sponsored by professional organizations, or professional seminars, for example. And be sure to read professional journals in your areas of interest to help you identify key players in that field.

Once you've done that, you can approach your contacts. Make sure that you state up-front that you're not asking them for a job! This is important; part of your "job" in the networking process is to make your contact comfortable. Don't worry that by stating you won't be asking them for a job you are closing things off—if there is a fit, your contact will let you know. Let them know that you just want to meet them and ask them for their input. Stick by your commitment to build the relationship rather than asking for a job and you'll be surprised how many doors those words will open for you.

When you do meet, ask yourself, and if appropriate, your contact, how you can be of use to him or her. This opens up the possibility of a real exchange.

Finally, you want to make good use of your and your contact's time, so have a plan for your meeting. The following pointers provide some guidance:

1. **Personalize the questions.** Break the ice by asking the contact about herself and her career. Possible questions: "You seem to really like your

job. How did you choose it?" "What is a typical day like for you?" "What are some of the most interesting projects you have worked on?"

2. **Show off your research.** Possible question: "I read that your firm is planning to expand in the next couple of years. What particular departments do you think the company will focus on growing?"
3. **Once you have established some rapport and learned about your contact's current job and career journey, broaden your questions to illicit information about her employer and the industry as a whole.** Possible questions: "What would you say are the hallmarks of this company?" "What unique qualities make it a good place to work?" "What changes have you seen in the industry over the past decade, and what do you see coming in the future?"
4. **Focus some of your questions on matters that will assist you with the nuts and bolts of your job search.** Possible questions: "Are there particular professional associations that people who hold your job typically join?" "How are jobs such as yours typically found?" "Are they advertised in particular trade journals, or are they found through word of mouth?"
5. **If the meeting has gone well and some rapport has been established, you might ask more pointed questions about applying to your contact's employer.** Possible questions: "Your company sounds like a great place to work. If I were to apply to your company at some point in the future, what would be the best process to

follow? Is there someone in particular to whom I should address application materials?"

6. **Do not ask the individual to put in a good word for you, or say anything else that makes it sound like you are asking them for a job.** Remember, you told them when you first contacted them that you wouldn't do so. If they offer to pass your résumé along or drop your name to a supervisor, great. But don't expect it. At this point in the process, they barely know you, so it's a lot to expect from them. Besides, chances are they are not the person in the organization in charge of hiring decisions. Your goal was to get helpful information from them, not a job.
7. **Always, always, always follow up with a formal "thank you" letter and offer to return the favor in the future if there is any way you can be of help to them.** And remember to check back in with your contact as your job search progresses and let them know how things are going.

Networking affords you the opportunity to learn about new people, new trends, new ideas, and a new way of life. Your life will take on a new shape through networking if you let it.

Career Comfort:

"People change in two ways—the books they read and the people they meet."
—Harvey Mackay

LESSON 35

COVER LETTERS ARE KEY

MANY PEOPLE SPEND HOURS ON THEIR résumés but ignore their cover letters. I review hundreds of résumés a month, but what influences headhunters and employers most when they decide whom to interview is the cover letter. Think about it. Résumés are incredibly awkward and difficult to read, even for those of us who work with them daily. But all too often, job seekers write a canned cover letter or simply toss in a cover sheet that says, "Enclosed please find my résumé."

Your cover letter is an opportunity to open a meaningful dialogue with a prospective employer and to demonstrate what you have to offer. It should reflect not only what skills you bring to the table, but also who you are as a person. So the lesson here is: whatever amount of time you spend writing your résumé, take three times that amount for your cover letter. Here are some basics to bear in mind:

BE CLEAR AND TO THE POINT

Keep your letter to one page and say only what you need to say:

1. What you know about the employer and the needs of the organization;
2. How your qualifications match those needs;
3. How you see the next step.

Demonstrate Your Research

Employers are impressed when it's evident that a candidate has taken time to get specific information about their organization. It sends the message that you're being selective and are not willing to work for just anyone. After stating why you're writing (e.g., someone referred you, you're responding to an ad, etc.), follow with your research using one to two sentences to highlight specific points.

> **For example:** *"I have followed the success of your organization over the last few years and am impressed by your growth rate of 55% over last year."*

Persuade

Follow your opening sentences with a recognition of the employer's needs. Then lead to your specific qualifications that match those needs.

> **For example:** *"My extensive experience in working with corporations and in-house counsel can benefit your bottom line by helping you cut your outside legal costs. Following are additional qualifications that I can bring to your organization:..." (Add three to four statements.)*

Closing Statement

Summarize the points of your letter and close with an open-ended statement that shows you're expecting an interview (rather than passively saying, "I'll wait for your call.").

> **For example:** *"It would seem in our mutual interests to further discuss the knowledge, experience and demonstrated results I can bring to your position. Thank you for your consideration. I look forward to a personal meeting to discuss this opportunity further."*

This method for writing cover letters can set you apart from your competition. It is personal, professional, and shows thought and preparation. Clients of ours who have previously not been considered for a position have repeatedly received greater interest from employers when using this cover letter format. So take the time to put some real thought into your cover letters—it works!

Exercise

- Make a list of at least five things that you want to reveal about yourself in your cover letter.
- Ask yourself: if I were standing in the employer's shoes, what would persuade them to meet with me?

Career Comfort:

I take the time to write a meaningful cover letter that sets me apart, and that is tailored to each job I apply for.

LESSON 36

Sharpen Your Most Valuable Tool: Your Résumé

YOUR COVER LETTER IS IN GOOD SHAPE now; how about your résumé? A truly effective résumé should not just provide the reader with a list of your experiences; it should persuade the reader that those experiences make you the right fit for the job. Brief, biographical résumés may have been sufficient in the past, but in a competitive market, substance is what will set you apart as a candidate.

Granted, it is difficult to objectively identify and isolate personal skills and separate yourself from other candidates whom you see as having similar experience. You may resist putting your qualifications down on paper, feeling they seem like an exaggeration when "I'm just doing my job." Rather than viewing your accomplishments as an exaggeration, however, think of your résumé as a persuasive document with you, the candidate, as the focus. Follow these four steps:

1. Start by writing, in narrative form, a description of your responsibilities (e.g., areas of expertise, work with clients, business development, management, technical, etc.).

2. Then, elaborate on your responsibilities by adding specific accomplishments. At this point, write as many as come to mind.

   For example:

   - Supervisors have acknowledged me for writing clear, concise memos that recognize their time constraints.
   - Clients have complimented me on my ability to translate complex information in a way that is easily understood.
   - I have been consistently recognized for my technical abilities in my area of expertise.

3. After writing several accomplishment statements, choose the accomplishments you wish to market to an employer. Then, using action verbs, quantify and/or qualify your statements.

   For example:

   Consistently recognized for expertise in resolving complex cases resulting in over 75 settlements in favor of corporate clients.

4. Now that you've identified your accomplishments, how do you put them in a résumé? The next step is to format a résumé and give it professional 'style.'

STYLE AND FORMAT

The following style offers a résumé that gets the attention of employers.

JOHN Q. DOE
100 Main Street
Anywhere, MN 55401
612-555-1111
John@esquiregroup.com

SUMMARY OF QUALIFICATIONS:

Follow with 2 to 3 specific highlights, e.g., "10 years experience specializing in the area of employment law."

PROFESSIONAL EXPERIENCE:

FIRM NAME - CITY, ST
Title: 1991- present

List employers in chronological order; include responsibilities and accomplishments

COMMUNITY SERVICE:

List volunteer activities

EDUCATION:

List graduate and undergraduate school, honors and extra curricular, e.g., Law Review or Phi Beta Kappa

PUBLICATIONS:

List any professional publications

PROFESSIONAL AFFILIATIONS:

List memberships and associations

Here are some style guidelines to consider:

Use **BOLD AND CAPS** for headings

Use ***bold and italics*** for highlights (e.g., ***cum laude, Law Review)***

Use underlines or *italics* for titles (e.g., senior accountant, manager, associate)

Gone are the days when a one page résumé is mandated. Unless you are new to the job market, two pages are standard these days. Three pages are often more than most employers want to read, but if the position is high level, it is often acceptable.

One effective way to get around overwhelming an employer with data is to prepare an addendum to your résumé. The addendum should list specific cases, matters, files or projects you have worked on. Arrange this information by topic for persuasive affect. For example, if you're a lawyer, you might list cases in your addendum by dollar amount, i.e., "$1 Million+ Verdicts," "$50,000+ Verdicts," etc. You could also arrange them by jurisdiction or by whether they were won on behalf of plaintiffs or defendants. If you are in the business world, you could arrange deals you've made by dollar amount, geographic location or type, such as "real estate deals," "mergers," "capital ventures," etc. The point is to provide greater detail than what is on your résumé, and to present it in such a way that convinces prospective employers you have both depth and breadth of experience in your field.

CAREER COMFORT:

I craft a résumé that persuades my prospective employer I am the right fit for the job.

LESSON 37

LESSONS FROM A HEADHUNTER... ABOUT HEADHUNTERS

SINCE I'M THE FOUNDER AND PRESIDENT of a search firm, it would be remiss of me not to offer some advice on this particular avenue in the job search process. I am often asked one of three questions: (1) What are the different types of search firms out there, (2) What type of search firm should I be working with, and (3) What is the best way to work with a search consultant.

Briefly, there are basically two different types of search firms: retained and contingent. How they work will often vary accordingly, so it's a good idea to know which type of firm you're dealing with prior to making contact.

1) THE TWO TYPES OF SEARCH FIRMS

Retained search firms are hired by an employer to fill a specific position. They typically are paid a portion of the fee up-front (i.e., a "retainer," which is typically one-third of the search fee), another third of the fee after ninety days from engagement, and the balance of the fee upon successful completion of the search. Most high level searches for CEOs, CFOs, General Counsel and other key hires are conducted on an exclusive, retained basis. Many of the large, international search firms work exclusively on a retained basis.

Conversely, contingent search firms are hired by an employer to fill a position but typically are not paid any fee upfront. They may or may not be working on a position exclusively, so it is a good idea to ask. Note that it won't hurt your candidacy to work with a firm that is not working on an exclusive basis. It is, however, important to assess how well informed they are on the position, and what their prior working relationship is with the employer, i.e., have they placed candidates there in the past, do they have access to and credibility with the decision-makers, how extensive are their networks in the fields you are looking in, etc. This is particularly important to ascertain in today's information age; the Internet has generated a whole new breed of "alleged search consultants" that simply go from company web page to company web page looking for positions to fill without being hired by the employer to do so. In short, there is no business relationship there; they are just hoping to find a candidate that will work. Again, you might find a job that way, but more often than not, I've seen candidates hurt rather than helped in such situations.

2) WHAT TYPE OF FIRM SHOULD YOU BE WORKING WITH

Why is all this important to *you*, the candidate? First and foremost, you need to recognize that with any search firm, the employer is the client as *they* are paying the fee for hiring you. This is not to say that you, the candidate, are not important to the search firm, but you are in essence the "product" that they would be presenting to the client.

Second, it's important as it relates to expectations you might have. Retained firms have historically been less interested in spending a lot of time fielding calls from candidates interested in making a career move. The majority of their time is typically spent seeking out candidates that fit the individual requirements for the search. In short, don't be offended if search consultants from retained firms don't take your call or respond to your résumé. It's just typically not their gig. I am not saying that you shouldn't make contact; just don't expect a response unless you fit one of the criteria for their current searches.

3) The Best Way to Work with A Search Consultant

The following seven tips will help you maximize your chances of building a successful relationship with a headhunter.

1. **Tell them what you want.** When first meeting with a search consultant, be sure to clearly describe the ideal position for you. This includes advising them of particular employers in whom you have an interest. When a consultant has a clear understanding of what makes you happy, they can expeditiously provide you with the right career choices. If you are unsure of what you want, let them know, as they may have other resources to help you.
2. **Advise them of your own search efforts.** To ensure that the consultant does not contact employers whom you have already contacted, remember to inform them which employers and, if possible, which particular persons at each employer, you have spoken with about job opportunities.
3. **Provide them with references, writing sam-**

ples, transcripts and addendums. Be prepared to provide the search consultant with a list of references and writing samples at the start. If an employer requests these materials from them (a common occurrence), they prefer to respond immediately without having to contact you again.

4. **Be accessible.** If you don't already have access to a computer with e-mail and/or an answering machine, I strongly advise you to purchase them so that you may regularly check for e-mail or voice mail messages. Opportunities happen quickly and can be lost if a recruiter can't locate you quickly.
5. **When scheduling interviews, be accomodating.** If an employer is interested in interviewing you, do all you can to accommodate the employer's preferred interview times. Flexibility sends a positive message.
6. **Debrief them immediately after each interview.** After interviewing with an employer, contact the consultant immediately and give them your feedback on how the interview went. After each interview, the employer is waiting to hear from the consultant and wants to know what you thought. If the employer has questions or concerns about your interview or candidacy, the consultant can end-run any potential problems.
7. **Be open.** The "ideal job" doesn't always look like it at first blush. If you are contacted for an interview, seriously consider it. I've found that once presented with an impressive candidate, an employer is often willing to amend a job description in order to make a good hire!

Career Comfort:

By being well informed, and having realistic expectations, I maximize my experience working with a headhunter and increase my chances of success.

LESSON 38

Rejection Is Only Feedback

YOU'VE SENT OUT YOUR RÉSUMÉS AND cover letters, or maybe they've been forwarded by a headhunter, and unfortunately so far you are underwhelmed by the response. In fact, you've experienced some outright rejection. Buddha taught that there is only pain in becoming "attached." When we feel rejected, we have allowed ourselves to be become attached to some predetermined outcome. In a job search, this typically shows up in getting attached to getting a particular interview or job offer.

When you're looking for work, you're especially vulnerable. You're putting yourself out there and taking risks. You want something, and when you don't get it, you feel pain. But no job, no boss, no client, no customer has power over you unless you give it to them. If someone says "no" to you, that doesn't make you a failure and it certainly doesn't mean you're not marketable. What it does mean is that this particular job isn't a good fit for you and it's time to move on. What you've received is feedback. It tells you that at this particular time you're not in the right place.

When employers share with me their reasons for not hiring someone, nine times out of ten, it's about the employer, not the candidate. Sometimes they want to see what other candidates are out there; sometimes they've gotten their hands slapped for not getting preapproval to hire. So don't think it's all about you! Be kind to yourself, and be realistic.

As the wonderfully creative artist/writer SARK says in one of her newsletters at www.planetsark.com, rejection just means that we're not reaching *far enough*, and therefore our job is to reach further.

But what if you heeded Lesson 10; you listened to your inner career coach and you were so convinced that the job you applied for *was* the right fit, yet you got rejected? What are the signals that you're the one case in ten when it really is about you? The answer is to look at where you are in the process and take in the feedback. If you routinely don't get interviews, you need to pay attention to this feedback. Typically that feedback is telling us there is a résumé or cover letter issue that needs addressing; maybe it's time to go back and re-visit Lessons 35 and 36. Conversely, if you are getting interviews but not receiving offers, it's likely that something is going on in the interview process that needs addressing. We'll tackle that in Lesson 41. The key here is to break it down and look at where your trouble spots are in the process.

You might also consider whether you're really ready for the job you're applying for. You may feel emotionally ready to make the change, but on an objective level, do you have the required credentials? There are times when you may need to take a step back and get additional training, or take a lower-level position to learn the ropes of the industry you've set your sights on, before moving upwards. The important thing in all this is to remember that if you resist feedback and continue doing things the way you've always done them, you'll continue getting the same results.

Career Comfort:

Rejection isn't a judgment about my worth or my marketability; it is merely feedback. If I pay attention to it, it will guide me where I need to go.

LESSON 39

Silence Is Golden

THE OPPOSITE OF LOVE, THEY SAY, ISN'T hate but indifference. When we hear nothing from prospective employers, the silence feels like indifference, and that can be excruciating.

If there is one thing I've learned after fifteen years of headhunting, it's how important it is not to attach too much meaning to the silence.

Before I became a headhunter, I couldn't understand why companies didn't respond to the résumés people sent. Now I know with 100% certainty that it's no reflection on the applicant. Rather, it usually reflects a lack of resources and time to respond on the part of the employer.

Silence is just silence. Don't let it make you doubt yourself. Instead, use the silence to attune yourself even more closely to your inner career coach.

Exercise

- If I'm experiencing silence, how can I use that silence to my advantage?
- If I take the time to become silent, what's my inner career coach telling me?

Career Comfort:

Silence allows me the time and space to think more about what's right for me.

LESSON 40

Patience Is Truly a Virtue

HAVE YOU INTERNALIZED THE PREVIOUS lesson on silence yet? Here's a related one. It's easy to get impatient when you're looking for a new job. But impatience is unproductive. Let's look at what's actually happening on the inside when we feel impatient. For most of us, it means we're focused on some event or point in the future, usually with some specific expectation in mind. We want the job offer, the raise, the promotion, and we want it now. Human? Yes. Helpful? No.

Impatience, by its very nature, implies that something is wrong in the present. This is a subtle form of negative thinking. You'll be far more productive, and ultimately more successful, in both your current job and your job search once you're able to stay focused on the present moment. This requires both discipline and trust—discipline with your thoughts and trust in your Higher Power, trust in the universe, and trust in the abundance you deserve.

Patience is really a form of surrender, and surrender can be excruciating for people who think control is what makes them successful. It's hard to accept the idea of surrender in our careers, because it demands that we turn over our will to our Higher Power; we have to accept that we can't will the job, the promotion or the raise into happening. But it also opens us up to the many possibilities the universe offers. It doesn't demand that we be able to name what we're learning; all we have to do is trust that something vital is being worked out in our world. We overcome our anxiety by surrendering, by turning it over to the Higher Power.

Career Comfort:

I stay in the present moment by surrendering; it is then that success comes to me.

LESSON 41

HAVE AN INTERVIEW AGENDA

YOU KNOW BY NOW THAT IT'S IMPORTANT to research a company and think about how you'll answer interview questions. But you can do more than this. It's incredibly powerful to step back and create your own agenda for an interview. Most people go into interviews thinking they're there to answer questions. They're shocked to find out they should be asking some questions of their own, and that they can and *should* play an active part in directing the course of the interview.

To determine your own agenda and take control of the interview process, pick three points that you want to get across to the interviewer. These can involve your work ethic, the experience you gained in a previous job, your willingness to travel and take on additional responsibility—anything.

To decide on the three points you want to get across during your interview, ask yourself the following questions:

- What do you want this person to know about you?

- What qualities does this job demand and which of those do you possess?
- What other things would be helpful for them to know about you?
- What attributes set you apart from other people who are interested in this job?
- What anecdotes or examples support the attributes you have chosen to share about yourself?

Some examples of the agenda points we have worked with candidates to develop include: what you have been consistently recognized for, what colleagues say about you, feedback from performance reviews, where you excel, why you are interested in this particular opportunity, and why you are a good fit for this particular position.

You can bring up your three agenda points up at any opportune time. They can even be a response to the worn-out interview question, "Tell me about yourself." I typically encourage my clients to let the interviewer take control initially, and then gently begin to shift control by saying something like, "There are a couple things I think it might helpful for you to know about me."

And don't forget the power of anecdotal answers. For each attribute or skill you want the interviewer to know about, make sure you have a specific example or story to support it. Anecdotes help convince your employer that you really do possess the skill you claim to have. Anyone can (and usually does) say, "I'm a people person." And answer like that becomes so much more effective if you immediately follow it up with a statement like, "Let me give you an example; in my current job I manage a very diverse group of 20 employees. Every one of them gave me high marks as an effective communicator and fair manager in my 360° review last year."

Anecdotes also make you more memorable – which is a real plus if the prospective employer is interviewing a sizeable string of candidates. Who would you, as an interviewer, remember more at the end of the day: a candidate who responds, succinctly, that she chose to become a lawyer because she "wanted to help people," or the candidate who in response to the same questions tells a short story about the selfless, hard-working lawyer in her home town who inspired her to follow in his footsteps?

Here are a few additional interview tips:

Do

1. Research the firm or company.
2. Wear a suit, have your shirt professionally cleaned, and shine your shoes. This holds true even for women. Although dresses and pant suits are acceptable in the workplace, a conservative suit is always your safest bet for an interview.
3. Make sure your pants are zipped! (Yes, this has actually happened.)
4. Practice your answers to difficult questions.
5. Be on time.
6. Mirror the handshake of your interviewer. If the interviewer has a firm handshake, return it in kind. If theirs is weak, don't overpower them with yours. Generally, people don't like either wet noodles or vise grips.
7. Admit that you're nervous if you are. Trying to hide it will only make it worse.
8. Be energetic and enthusiastic.
9. Sell yourself. This is not the time to be modest. Give the employer a reason to get excited about you.

10. Make eye contact with your interviewer.
11. Ask good questions.
12. Get across your agenda. Talk about your strong points even if you are not asked about them directly.
13. Be as flexible as possible when talking about your availability to start this position.
14. Send a thank-you letter to each person with whom you met, and make sure you get the correct spelling of each person's name.

DON'T

1. Don't wear cologne or perfume.
2. Don't smoke immediately before the interview.
3. Don't wear trendy or casual clothing. This is not the time to try out your tie with the cartoon characters emblazoned on it!
4. Don't assume that the interview is merely a formality. Always sell yourself.
5. Don't talk about dissatisfaction with your current job or career.
6. Don't complain about your current employer. Express your reasons for leaving as a positive statement of what you are looking for, not a negative statement of what you want to get away from.
7. Don't interrupt the interviewer.
8. Don't talk too much or too little. The best interviews are always a two-way conversation between you and the interviewer.
9. Don't fidget. If you tend to fidget and play with objects such as your pen or a paper clip, don't tempt

yourself. Place your (empty) hands on your lap and keep them still.

10. Don't talk about money until the employer raises the issue.
11. Don't use foul language.
12. Don't discuss inappropriate personal matters. Remember, this is a business meeting. Although an employer wants to get to know you personally to determine if you will work well together, they do not want to know about your current personal problems.
13. Don't make remarks inappropriate to the environment. For example, don't refer to yourself as a "maverick" if you are interviewing for a position in a conservative corporation.

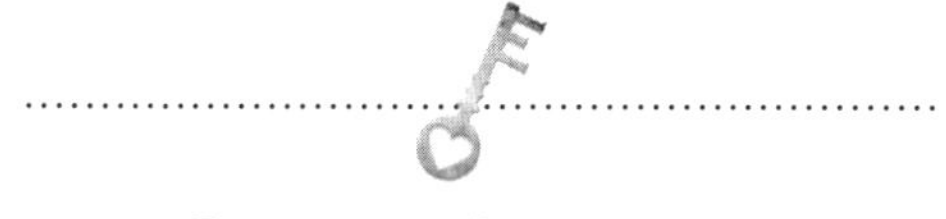

CAREER COMFORT:

I will have a game plan and willingly take an active role in determining the course of the interview.

LESSON 42

DON'T JUST SAY NO

WE'RE NOT FINISHED WITH THE TOPIC OF interview preparation quite yet! I credit this lesson to one of my mentors, Carolyn Brown, a seasoned search consultant with over twenty years in the business.

Interviewers will often ask if you have experience doing something you've never done. Don't try to bluff your way or exaggerate what you've done to fit the task. Instead, be honest. Saying "no" is not fatal. In fact, the prospective employer will respect you for your honesty and professionalism. You'll build trust and rapport, and that's a worthwhile accomplishment in an interview.

But don't *just* say no. Let's say you're asked, "Have you ever managed employees?" You've never done that, but you have managed projects, deadlines and outside vendor relationships. So you reply, "No, I have not managed employees who were direct reports. However, I have managed the people who comprise our outside vendor relationships, and I have managed people within the context of project completion and meeting deadlines." Bingo, you've just described relevant experience and opened up a whole new avenue of discussion.

Just remember, the examples you use have to be relevant and meaningful to the employer. It won't work if they're not on point.

Career Comfort:

Even if I haven't performed a particular job requirement, I know how to sell myself in an honest, meaningful way.

LESSON 43

PAY ATTENTION TO HOW YOU'RE TREATED

THROUGHOUT EACH OF THE "DOING" steps discussed so far, you need to stay not only actively engaged, but *observant.* If you've had a bad experience with a past employer or have more than one job offer and are wrestling with which one to take, I encourage you to pay attention to how you are, or were, treated in the interview process. It can tell you a lot about the organization.

I'm not saying that you absolutely shouldn't take the job if the employer rescheduled your interview three times, or you had to wait longer than you expected to get your benefits packet from Human Resources. But do pay attention to what happens throughout the entire interview and offer process because it will tell you a lot about the core values (or lack thereof) of the organization, and may give you a glimpse into the future of your relationship with them.

It's particularly important to pay close attention to whatever you learn about an organization at this stage of the process, because you're not going to be change the organization. You might be able to influence it or effect some limited change within your department, but you're not going to make the organization into something different.

Likewise, it's easy to get off track and be so swayed by the great personality of one interviewer, or so dazzled by the swanky office space, that you ignore any red flags. If it's one impressive individual in the organization who is influencing your decision, remember that he or she could take another job tomorrow and you'd be left with the organization. It happens a lot!

This is the time to revisit Lesson 25; make sure that the "soul of the job" is consistent with how you were treated throughout the recruitment process. What you're trying to avoid is jumping at the first thing that comes along, and ignoring the warning signs along the way. The most common reason we do that is, of course, anxiety about the job search process and fear that this may be the only offer we get. This is when you need to remind yourself to trust your Higher Power that the right job will come to you. For more help with learning to trust, continue the work you started in Lesson 19.

The knee-jerk reaction to take a job can also keep you from thinking clearly in the negotiation process, and hinder you from getting the money, benefits or other important perks that you deserve. Negotiating makes many of us uncomfortable in the first place, so it's particularly important to have a well thought-out game plan in advance; the next lesson will give you some more insight on negotiating.

And be advised: employers often take a long time to make an offer and then expect you to make a decision right away. Stay in a decision-making mode throughout the process. Don't think you can take as long as you want to decide about an offer when it comes. Be ready.

Career Comfort:

I am watching for all the signs along the way in my job search process, and will use them to make good decisions about the job that is right for me.

LESSON 44

Life Is a Series of Negotiations

A FRIEND OF MINE ONCE TOLD ME THAT she hated shopping in the open air markets of Mexico. I was surprised—she has decorated her entire home with Mexican art and I would have guessed she'd see the markets as a bonanza of bargains. "I don't like to negotiate with the shopkeepers," she explained. "I just want to pay a set price and be done with it. It just doesn't feel right to negotiate."

Many candidates feel the same way in the job search process. But I will tell you right now, you will have to negotiate if you want to ultimately achieve job satisfaction. It will be expected of you, and you owe it to yourself. It is, in fact, one of the acts of "self-love" I talked about in Lesson 7 and an important way to take care of yourself.

So how do you gear up for negotiating? There are entire books written on what to say, how to say it, and when to say it, but I have found the biggest hurdle is accepting that you should in fact engage in negotiation, and giving yourself permission to do it.

As with many of the doctrines we have discussed so far, one of the most important steps is to find your own style. You do not have to have the razor-sharp claws and killer instinct of a Donald Trump. Don't become someone else when it's time to negotiate.

Second, only negotiate when it feels right. That doesn't mean don't push yourself to do it; it means knowing what signs to watch for. For example, is your prospective employer a lock-step environment, that is, do they pay everyone at the same seniority level the same, pre-set salary? If so, then not only will it be futile to attempt to negotiate your salary, but you will look naïve at best, and undermine your credibility or irritate your employer at worst. This is where your network can help you; is there someone in your network who knows about the internal workings of this particular company, or has engaged in salary negotiations with a similar employer?

Bear in mind also that there is a lot more than salary to negotiate, such as office space, the technology at your disposal, vacation, budget to carry out your duties (i.e., travel or marketing budget), support staff, number of direct reports, or where your position falls in the reporting hierarchy. Benefits may also be negotiable, but mind the advice on salary negotiation above—some benefits aspects may not be negotiable and you'll do yourself more harm than good by attempting to open up that discussion. Generally, those benefits that broadly impact others in the company and are tied to contracts with outside vendors, such as the amount of co-pay on your company health insurance, are generally fixed. Benefits that are more specific to particular jobs within the organization, such as an allowance for continuing education, are more likely to have an aspect of flexibility.

The bottom line is that you must accept that negotiation of some kind *will* be a part of securing your next position. It is less daunting when you realize that you already negotiate every day, on the job and off, and you've probably already had success at it. Any time we engage in an exchange of goods or power, we are negotiating. Have you ever offered to watch your neighbor's kids on Friday night, if she'll watch yours next Saturday night? Did she agree? Then you negotiated successfully. Did you ever tell your boss that you would stay late every night next week if you could *please* take tomorrow off? Did the boss acquiesce? See, you do it more than you know!

Finally, recognize that many employers will fully expect you to negotiate, and will in fact be forming initial impressions of you, based on how you handle yourself during the offer and acceptance phase. This is particularly true if have applied for a position in areas like law, business, finance, or sales, where negotiating is actually part of the job description. This is not to say that you should negotiate for the sake of negotiating. There's no need to squabble about the minutia just to prove that you are a real barracuda. Save it for those aspects of the position that will make a real difference in your long-term satisfaction. But rest assured that a prospective employer will *not* think you ungrateful or difficult if you respectfully ask, "Is that part of the offer open for discussion?"

Career Comfort:

I give myself permission to negotiate; it is an act of self-love that will ensure my long-term satisfaction. I know that I do not need to become someone else in order to negotiate effectively.

LESSON 45

WHY COUNTEROFFERS ARE COUNTERPRODUCTIVE

YOU KNOW WHAT THE BOY SCOUTS say—be prepared. Your résumé is out there, and you're getting interviews. It won't be long before you get an offer for a position that means more money, a better situation, and new opportunities. You'll give notice that you are leaving your current employer. It's very possible that your boss will then say, "Tell me what they offered. I'll match it or beat it." How will you handle that curve ball?

Before jumping at a counteroffer, it is my advice to think long and hard. Ask yourself this: If you were worth X dollars yesterday, why is your company suddenly willing to pay you Y dollars today? Obviously there were reasons you were unhappy and wanted to change—have those actually changed? Accepting a counteroffer can have numerous negative consequences. Consider these Top 10 reasons to say "no" to a counteroffer.

Reason No. 1:

What type of company do you work for if you must threaten to resign before they give you what you are worth?

Reason No. 2:

Where is the money for the counteroffer coming from? Is it your next raise, early? (Many companies have strict wage and salary guidelines that must be followed.)

Reason No. 3:

Your company will immediately start looking for a new person at a lower salary.

Reason No. 4:

You have now made your employer aware that you are unhappy. From this day on, your loyalty will be in question.

Reason No. 5:

When promotion time comes around, your employer will remember who was loyal and who wasn't. Which list do you think you will be on?

Reason No. 6:

When times get tough, your employer could begin the cutbacks with you.

Reason No. 7:

The same circumstances that now cause you to consider a change will repeat themselves in the future, even if you accept a counteroffer. Are you just delaying the inevitable?

Reason No. 8:

Statistics compiled by the National Employment Association confirm that over 80% of those people who elected to accept a counteroffer are not with their company six months later.

Reason No. 9:

Accepting a counteroffer often feels like a bribe and a blow to your personal pride. Were you bought?

Reason No. 10:

Once the word gets out, the relationship that you now enjoy with your coworkers will never be the same. You may well lose the personal satisfaction of peer group acceptance.

One of the best ways to avoid the counteroffer trap is to be honest with yourself and understand your motivations even *before* you begin exploring your employment options. Recording and focusing on your motivations allows you to better evaluate opportunities and provides you with a concrete reminder of what is really important to you in a career. For example, if you are happy with every aspect of your current position except for your level of compensation, and your motivation for seeking a new job offer is to position yourself for a counteroffer, you should reevaluate your decision. In short, be sure that your intention to make a change is sincere and not an attempt to elicit a raise from your current employer.

Finally, don't succumb to "emotional blackmail" when your employer begs you to stay. You began a job search for a reason. Before accepting a counteroffer (and possibly reneging on your acceptance of your new position), again consider why you began looking for a different job in the first place, and why you accepted your new position. Looking back on your written list of motivating factors will help you stay strong when your current employer tries to lay a guilt trip on you.

Career Comfort:

I protect myself in a counteroffer situation by remaining mindful of what led me to seek a new position in the first place.

LESSON 46

RESIGN IN STYLE

YOU HAVE NEARLY REACHED THE END OF your journey and are ready to start another. As they say, there is nothing like starting with a clean slate. When it comes to beginning a new job, the best way to ensure your slate is sparkling clean is to leave no loose ends at your former place of employment, and, more important, to *not* burn any bridges. That can be tough. It's hard to keep focusing on your present job when mentally and emotionally you've already moved on to the next. Moreover, sometimes the negative circumstances that have caused us to seek new employment tempt us to pull a few dirty little tricks on our way out the door—like hiding an important file, or giving only a few days notice in hopes of experiencing the "thrill" of leaving your former employer in a lurch. As much fun as those scenarios may be to daydream about, I am begging you, let them be daydreams only. Do not act on those impulses.

"Why not?" you may be asking. "I'm never going to have anything to do with this employer ever again, right?" Maybe. But most likely, you will. We talked a lot back in the networking chapters about how small the world is. Odds are, you will run into your former employer again, particularly if your new job is in the same or a related industry. You may run into a former co-worker or boss at conventions or other professional events, or serve together on association committees. You may sit with them on the board of directors of a community organization. Your former employer may end up being a client, provider, vendor or partner of your current company. (I have seen this happen to many lawyers who end up being co-counsel, or opposing counsel, on a matter with someone from their former law office.) And even though you may not believe it now, there may come a day where you need a reference from your soon-to-be former employer for yet another job change. In short, it's very likely you will rub elbows with someone from your former work life some day, and maybe even need a favor from them.

So how do you resign in style? Follow these five basic steps:

1. **Give plenty of notice.** What constitutes appropriate notice varies from industry to industry. In some fields, the basic two weeks is standard. In others, such as law or executive level positions where it takes longer to transition your files to someone else and notify clients, four weeks or more is common. Find out what is acceptable in your field.
2. **Offer to help find your replacement.** Your resignation will probably throw your boss and your coworkers into a panic, wondering how they will cover your workload. You will be a hero if you offer to help spread the word about your position and put your employer in touch with potential candidates. You may be thinking, "But I am leaving this job/workplace because I didn't like it, so why would I want to encourage a colleague to come work

here?" If that's the case, you can at least provide your employer with tips on what industry publications and web sites people in your position tend to read, so your employer can advertise the newly open position there.

3. **Write a professional letter of resignation.** It should be short and succinct. While you needn't be insincerely effusive, or sugarcoat things—don't say it was the best job you've ever had if it most decidedly was not—at least be diplomatic. If there are ills that you feel you simply must expose for the good of the organization, or if there are things you have to get off your chest for the sake of your emotional health, request an exit interview. Exit interviews are typically standard procedure following a resignation anyway. But even there, don't resort to finger-pointing or name-calling. Keep your comments honest but constructive.
4. **Leave detailed instructions.** Write an exit memo letting coworkers or supervisors know where to find your files and where you are in terms of pending projects. Include contact information for key individuals outside the organization with whom you interact regularly. Make everyone on the team aware of upcoming deadlines, and obviously, finish up as many matters as you can before you go.
5. **Thank your employer.** Remember in Lesson 2 we talked about how no matter how negative of an experience a job turns out to be, there is always something you can learn from that job, and always some skill you can take from it to add to your tool kit. Find that thing, and thank your employer for it. And remember to bless your Higher Power for the old job as well as the new.

In short, though it's a tempting fantasy, at no time should the phrase, "Take this job and shove it," ever leave your mouth during your last days of employment. Take the high road and maintain your professionalism. It will be your legacy as you exit this job...and it will come back to haunt you if you don't. The principle of negative energy attracting more negative energy applies on your last day of work just as much—and perhaps even more so—as on any other day of your journey so far.

Career Comfort:

I will maintain my professionalism and integrity throughout the resignation process.

Let's Recap...

Can you believe how far you've come since you first acknowledged that nagging, little thought in the back of your mind, "I'm not happy in my job"? You've made the tough decision to move on, you've toppled barriers that it took a lifetime to build, you've envisioned where you want to end up, and you've filled your tool kit with all the tools you need to find, get, evaluate and negotiate for, the right job. The prize is almost within your grasp; you can and will see this through. Keep the Career Comforts you've worked so hard to realize foremost in your mind. Pull them out whenever you need them, and you will stay true to your path until the end. I wish you all the best.

Career Comforts for Doing

Career Comfort:

I will write a job sculpting proposal that meets my goals and makes sense for my employer. I recognize that I have to take the lead in making the re-sculpting happen.

Career Comfort:

Networking is what I make of it; I determine whether or not it's an imposition on others by the way I choose to go about it.

Career Comfort:

"People change in two ways—the books they read and the people they meet."—Harvey Mackay

Career Comfort:

I take the time to write a meaningful cover letter that sets me apart, and that is tailored to each job I apply for.

Career Comfort:

I craft a résumé that persuades my prospective employer I am the right fit for the job.

Career Comfort:

By being well informed, and having realistic expectations, I maximize my experience working with a headhunter and increase my chances of success.

Career Comfort:

Rejection isn't a judgment about my worth or my marketability; it is merely feedback. If I pay attention to it, it will guide me where I need to go.

Career Comfort:

Silence allows me the time and space to think more about what's right for me.

Career Comfort:

I stay in the present moment by surrendering; it is then that success comes to me.

Career Comfort:

I will have a game plan and willingly take an active role in determining the course of the interview.

Career Comfort:

Even if I haven't performed a particular job requirement, I know how to sell myself in an honest, meaningful way.

Career Comfort:

I am watching for all the signs along the way in my job search process, and will use them to make good decisions about the job that is right for me.

Career Comfort:

I give myself permission to negotiate; it is an act of self-love that will ensure my long-term satisfaction. I know that I do not need to become someone else in order to negotiate effectively.

Career Comfort:

I protect myself in a counteroffer situation by remaining mindful of what led me to seek a new position in the first place.

Career Comfort:

I will maintain my professionalism and integrity throughout the resignation process.

Complete Collection of Career Comforts

Career Comforts for Contemplating

Career Comfort:

Because I have a choice in what I believe, I am not stuck. I take care of myself, I have the freedom to make choices, and I have the ability to create the work life I want.

Career Comfort:

I bless this job and thank my Higher Power for sending it to me when I needed it. I am choosing to lovingly release it and pass it on to the next person who needs it. I now choose to move on to a position that meets my needs and helps me fulfill what is best in me.

Career Comfort:

People grow and change; if my job has not grown with me, I have the ability to choose a job that is right for me now.

Career Comfort:

I exercise my free will in my job search because I am in the best position to determine what is right for me.

Career Comfort:

I have options to consider other than leaving my job immediately.

Career Comfort:

I will know when I am ready and I will wait until then to take appropriate action.

Career Comfort:

I can trust what's right for me, and I can leave my job whenever the time is right for me.

Career Comfort:

I choose to say yes to all good, all opportunity and all blessings. I choose to turn away from my own negativity and the negativity of others.

Career Comfort:

Listening to my pain will bring me to a new awareness of my values and aspirations. I have nothing to fear.

Career Comfort:

My inner career coach guides me safely to my right path and mission. I open myself to the wisdom inside of me.

Career Comforts for Overcoming

Career Comfort:

I can choose to continue important relationships outside of the work environment, or reconfigure those relationships. I can redefine myself as an individual or as part of a new team.

Career Comfort:

I am a multi-faceted person. With or without my current job, I will continue to be me.

Career Comfort:

I can trust my inner career coach—my job is to listen to it and to discern it from the voices of others.

Career Comfort:

It's natural for me to feel a sense of loss. My way through the loss is through trust. I trust that the right job is coming to me now.

Career Comfort:

I can easily turn around my limiting beliefs.

Career Comfort:

How much money I truly need is based almost entirely on my own perceptions. I have the power to change my perceptions if I choose.

Career Comfort:

I choose to believe that prosperity is my right and comes to me easily.

Career Comfort:

I determine what prosperity means to me, and I think creatively about how to achieve my definition of prosperity.

Career Comfort:

I am safe and secure. No harm can come to me. I am worthwhile and my right work comes to me in the right place and at the right time.

Career Comfort:

"We have nothing to fear but fear itself."
—Franklin Delano Roosevelt

Career Comfort:

I recognize that job searching by its very nature involves promoting myself and my abilities, and I can learn to become comfortable with that.

Career Comfort:

I decide what career is right for me based on my skills, abilities, and interests, as opposed to outdated societal norms. I do not have to bear the sole burden of providing for my family.

Career Comfort:

There is no need to compete because there is enough to go around. All I have to do is demonstrate my own gifts and talents, and how I would exercise them in my own unique way.

Career Comfort:

I will use this time to rethink my career path. I will not allow myself to take this termination as a comment on my personal worth. I am thankful for what I have learned through this process, and I will apply it as I move ahead into my next job.

Career Comforts for Planning

Career Comfort:

Throughout my job transition, I will remain clearly focused on the soul of the job I am seeking and I will let it determine my path.

Career Comfort:

I take ownership of my happiness, and I look for a work life that will allow me to experience some of the same happiness in the workplace that I experience in other areas of my life. I give myself permission to enjoy my work.

Career Comfort:

I deserve to have the jobs that I am applying for; I am qualified and ready to make my own unique contribution.

Career Comfort:

I don't need to do this alone, nor should I.

Career Comfort:

I have the power to reinvent myself. I understand that more radical job change brings with it more risks, but I am ready to face those risks, knowing that they can reap great rewards.

Career Comfort:

I will not use education as a haven from the real world. I am ready to go out into the workplace and test the skills I have been trained to use.

Career Comfort:

I will take care of myself and get help if I need it. Only then can I truly move forward.

Career Comforts for Doing

Career Comfort:

I will write a job sculpting proposal that meets my goals and makes sense for my employer. I recognize that I have to take the lead in making the re-sculpting happen.

Career Comfort:

Networking is what I make of it; I determine whether or not it's an imposition on others by the way I choose to go about it.

Career Comfort:

"People change in two ways—the books they read and the people they meet."
—Harvey Mackay

Career Comfort:

I take the time to write a meaningful cover letter tailored to each job I apply for.

Career Comfort:

I craft a résumé that persuades my prospective employer I am the right fit for the job.

Career Comfort:

By being well informed, and having realistic expectations, I maximize my experience working with a headhunter and increase my chances of success.

Career Comfort:

Rejection isn't a judgment about my worth or my marketability; it is merely feedback and if I pay attention to it, it will guide me where I need to go.

Career Comfort:

Silence allows me the time and space to think more about what's right for me.

Career Comfort:

I stay in the present moment by surrendering; it is then that success comes to me.

Career Comfort:

I will have a game plan and willingly take an active role in determining the course of the interview.

Career Comfort:

Even if I haven't performed a particular job requirement, I know how to sell myself in an honest, meaningful way.

Career Comfort:

I am watching for all the signs along the way in my job search process, and will use them to make good decisions about the job that is right for me.

Career Comfort:

I give myself permission to negotiate; it is an act of self-love that will ensure my long-term satisfaction. I know that I do not need to become someone else in order to negotiate effectively.

Career Comfort:

I protect myself in a counteroffer situation by remaining mindful of what led me to seek a new position in the first place.

Career Comfort:

I will maintain my professionalism and integrity throughout the resignation process.